TRANSACTIONS

OF THE

AMERICAN PHILOSOPHICAL SOCIETY

HELD AT PHILADELPHIA
FOR PROMOTING USEFUL KNOWLEDGE

NEW SERIES—VOLUME 66, PART 7
1976

RECURRENT THEMES AND SEQUENCES IN NORTH AMERICAN INDIAN-EUROPEAN CULTURE CONTACT

EDWARD McM. LARRABEE

THE AMERICAN PHILOSOPHICAL SOCIETY
INDEPENDENCE SQUARE
PHILADELPHIA

November, 1976

WITHDRAWN

PUBLICATIONS

OF

The American Philosophical Society

The publications of the American Philosophical Society consist of PROCEEDINGS, TRANSACTIONS, MEMOIRS, and YEAR BOOK.

THE PROCEEDINGS contains papers which have been read before the Society in addition to other papers which have been accepted for publication by the Committee on Publications. In accordance with the present policy one volume is issued each year, consisting of six bimonthly numbers, and the price is $8.00 net per volume.

THE TRANSACTIONS, the oldest scholarly journal in America, was started in 1769 and is quarto size. In accordance with the present policy each annual volume is a collection of monographs, each issued as a part. The current annual subscription price is $20.00 net per volume. Individual copies of the TRANSACTIONS are offered for sale.

Each volume of the MEMOIRS is published as a book. The titles cover the various fields of learning; most of the recent volumes have been historical. The price of each volume is determined by its size and character.

The YEAR BOOK is of considerable interest to scholars because of the reports on grants for research and to libraries for this reason and because of the section dealing with the acquisitions of the Library. In addition it contains the Charter and Laws, and lists of present and former members, and reports of committees and meetings. The YEAR BOOK is published about April 1 for the preceding calendar year. The current price is $5.00.

An author desiring to submit a manuscript for publication should send it to the Editor, George W. Corner, American Philosophical Society, 104 South Fifth Street, Philadelphia, Pa. 19106.

TRANSACTIONS

OF THE

AMERICAN PHILOSOPHICAL SOCIETY

HELD AT PHILADELPHIA
FOR PROMOTING USEFUL KNOWLEDGE

NEW SERIES—VOLUME 66, PART 7
1976

RECURRENT THEMES AND SEQUENCES IN NORTH AMERICAN INDIAN-EUROPEAN CULTURE CONTACT

EDWARD McM. LARRABEE

THE AMERICAN PHILOSOPHICAL SOCIETY
INDEPENDENCE SQUARE
PHILADELPHIA

November, 1976

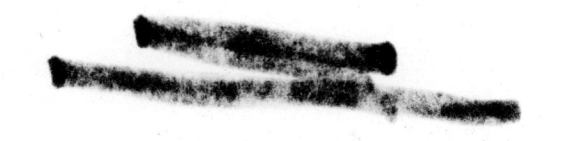

Copyright © 1976 by The American Philosophical Society

Library of Congress Catalog
Card Number 76-24257
International Standard Book Number 0-87169-667-3
US ISSN 0065-9746

RECURRENT THEMES AND SEQUENCES IN NORTH AMERICAN INDIAN–EUROPEAN CULTURE CONTACT

Edward McM. Larrabee

CONTENTS

I. Introduction	3
II. Description of the "Brotherton" Reservation	3
The situation in New Jersey up to the 1750's	3
The French and Indian War	7
The creation and maintenance of Brotherton	11
Liquidation of the community	16
III. Relevant themes	18
Themes in Delaware culture	18
Coincident themes jointly shared in Lenape and Anglo-American cultures	19
Themes in Anglo-American culture	20
IV. Problems interfering with expression of these themes	22
Conflict in Delaware cultural themes	22
Conflict in area of shared values	23
Conflict in Anglo-American cultural themes	24
Discussion of diagram of "Thermal Interaction"	25
V. Parallels and sequence	27
Identification of parallels	27
Generalized sequence of cultural interaction	30
Comments on sequence	32
Uses of the model	38
VI. Analysis of interaction of cultural themes	39
Themes common to native North American cultures	39
Themes coincident to Indian and Euro-American culture	40
Themes common to Euro-American culture	40
Themes which have emerged as the intercultural relationship developed	41
Bibliography	44
Index	49

I. INTRODUCTION

Study of a relatively little known eighteenth-century attempt to create a "reservation" for a remnant group of Delaware Indians in central New Jersey has revealed a number of striking parallels between this sequence of events and subsequent federal dealings with other groups of Native Americans. So many parallels exist that the New Jersey sequence is almost like a preview in miniature of the problems of culture-contact between Anglo-Americans and Indians in the United States. This paper will briefly describe the story of the reservation, with emphasis on the expressions of attitudes and the appearance of problems during the creation, maintenance, and final liquidation of the community which have later parallels. It will then attempt to explain the similarities by identifying certain continuing themes in the participant cultures, and in the relationship between them. Such an explicitly inductive process duplicates the questions raised in the author's mind when he started to describe and analyze "Brotherton," and found repeated similarities to other long-term culture-contact events. The explanatory sequence of cultural interaction in the latter part of the paper represents an attempt to answer those questions.

Two things should be mentioned before we examine the specific data and try to draw general explanations. The first of these is the mass of recent Indian material, both popular and scholarly, which has appeared in print and in public entertainment. The popular material, particularly, has tended toward a certain amount of romanticizing of Indians, and condemnation of Whites. Since my aim here is to understand the relationship between two or more cultures, including their respective value system, it would obscure the analysis to apply my own value judgments prematurely. The second matter concerns priority. It has been claimed by local historians that "Brotherton" was the first Indian reservation in what is now the United States (Allinson, 1875: p. 45n; DeCou, 1932; Bisbee, 1971: p. 116; New Jersey Bell, 1974). Probaby some of the "Indian Towns" of Massachusetts Bay Colony in the seventeenth century are sufficiently similar in intent or practical effects so that they can be considered earlier manifestations of the same phenomena (Vaughan, 1965; Leach, 1966). What is important is not that the attempt in New Jersey was the very first example, but that it did occur relatively early, was not directly connected to later and larger culture-contact situations, and yet contained elements remarkably similar to the subsequent development of what came to be called "the Indian Problem" by Anglo-American writers and officials.

II. DESCRIPTION OF THE "BROTHERTON" RESERVATION

THE SITUATION IN NEW JERSEY UP TO THE 1750'S

New Jersey and the immediately adjacent portions of surrounding states were inhabited in the early seventeenth century by Delawaran-speaking peoples (a language of the Algonquian group) who shared a similar culture, and referred to themselves as "Lenape," and were not unified in an overall political sense (Newcomb, 1956), but may have been organized into polities large enough to encompass many residence groups, perhaps in three or more "tribes" (Thurman, 1974). Their livelihood was based on maize-beans-squash and other crops grown in gardens tended by the women and on vegetal matter they collected, on fish and game obtained by the men, and on seashore resources. The gathering of all this subsistence and caring for plants produced a seasonal pattern of movement within limited areas, including one or more communal hunts. Evidently the tendency was for uxorilocal residence and matrilineal descent in families which were grouped, on a wider geographic basis, into "lineages" (Wallace, 1947: p. 6). Villages numbering from fifty to two hundred people, and consisting of one or more lineages, were common, and the estimated total population in pre-contact times was perhaps on the order of ten thousand (Mooney, 1911: p. 333; 1928: p. 4; Kroeber, 1947: p. 140; Newcomb, 1956: p. 10; Weslager, 1972: pp. 34–37). It is possible that control of larger territories was through a patrilineal system (Wallace, 1949: p. 8).

Regular contact with Europeans began shortly after 1600, and by 1640 trade and land purchase were established institutions, and warfare had occurred between people whose descendants a century later were considered Delaware Indians, and Dutch and Swedes on the Delaware, and Dutch on the Hudson (Acrelius, 1876; Ruttenber, 1872; Johnson, 1911; Huston, 1950; Leiby, 1964; McMahon, 1971).

Following this initial period of contact the Delawaran people had little or no direct conflict with the various European colonists, all of whom were under English rule after 1664. They were, however, affected by disease, and by the intense fur-trade wars fought among the northeast woodland Indians, from which the Iroquois emerged supreme near the end of the seventeenth century (Hunt, 1940). By and large, they did not suffer the wholesale displacements, migrations, and destruction which were the fate of other groups such as the Mohican, Susquehanna, Huron, or Erie (Hunt, 1940; Hoffman, n.d., 1964). By 1680 the Delawaran people were considerably reduced in number, and were under some sort of subservience to the Iroquois (A. F. C. Wallace, 1947, 1949; P. A. W. Wallace, 1945, 1961; Weslager, 1972). This may be the first situation in which the Lenape were treated as a group, which became important in that it tended to make them think of themselves as such. Newcomb thinks that "consolidation" occurred effectively during the first half of the eighteenth century (1956: pp. 84–87), although others argue that several tribal groups which together encompassed all the Delaware people may already have existed (Hunter, 1974 b: pp. 147–48; Jennings, 1974: pp. 91–92; Thurman, 1974: pp. 112, 123, 127–28). It is important, however, to note that Newcomb was referring to the main body of Delawares, who were migrating west in a piecemeal fashion, first to northeast and central Pennsylvania and then to the Ohio country, during this period. There were several hundreds left in small groups in central New Jersey, and it is with these that we are concerned (Weslager, 1972: pp. 261–263).

The land which became New Jersey was divided by English royal charter into East and West Jersey, and conveyed to proprietors, who became the holders and sellers of land and promoters of colonization (Tanner, 1908; Fisher, 1911; Pomfret, 1964). Both the East and West Jersey Boards of Proprietors seem to have made a fairly consistent effort to extinguish "native title" by purchasing the land claims of Indians. The situation was complicated by the attempts of some private parties to circumvent the claims of the proprietors, and buy directly from Indians. As will be seen, there were evidently some exceptions in practice, in cases where the Indian vendors felt that they had been cheated by agreements reached after they had been made drunk, or by payments not made as promised. There were also certain tracts of land for which some Indians who claimed an interest were not paid, although in some of these cases other Indians had been paid. We could introduce here the problem of what sort of concepts existed among the Lenape concerning the ownership and alienability of land (Heckewelder, 1881: p. 102; Speck, 1915; Lowie, 1920; McLeod, 1922; A. F. C. Wallace, 1947; Newcomb, 1956). Probably at first the Indians who had an inherited interest in the territory in which their kin group hunted and collected intended to make a grant of shared use in that area to the Europeans with whom they dealt, in exchange for gifts from the Europeans (A. F. C. Wallace, 1947: p. 2). Undoubtedly as increasing areas of land became unusable to them because of European activities, and the number of sales and of Europeans accumulated and the number of Indians decreased, the remaining Delawares developed different concepts. For our purposes, the important fact is that there was dissatisfaction on the part of the Lenape over some sales which had been made, and, in addition, some of them felt that there were specific tracts which they had never sold, but which were now occupied by Europeans.

This dissatisfaction was not, however, of great moment to the Anglo-American inhabitants of New Jersey in the first half of the eighteenth century, nor to the elected Assembly which represented them. There had been no Indian wars since the Dutch days, and most of the Indians had disappeared either through disease or migration to Pennsylvania. While treaties, conferences, and Indian relations were of vital interest to the colonies of New York and Pennsylvania (Uhler, 1951; Larrabee, n.d.,b; Trelease, 1960), New Jersey was simply unconcerned. In 1748 and again in 1754 Johnathan Belcher, royal governor of New Jersey, futilely urged the Assembly to support or participate in general treaty conferences being held at Albany between the north central British colonies and the Iroquois (*N. J. Archives* 7: p. 149; 16: pp. 455–458, 474–477; N. J. Assembly Journal 8 July, 1748). The governor had to report to the Lords of Trade that he found "by the publick Records of the Province" that the Assembly "never would concern themselves, or join in such Treaties" (*N. J. Archives* 8: Part I: p. 191).

At a more local level, however, there was concern among the Anglo-American colonists, at least when they felt threatened by the presence of too large a group of Indians. There were still some Delawares of the northern group (the Munsi, resident on the upper Delaware River) in the province, but they were not directly involved in the events which resulted in the creation of the Brotherton reservation. The center of the province had been inhabited by the Unami, the main division of the Lenape (Newcomb, 1956: pp. 5–7; Hunter, 1961: p. 2; 1974 *b*: p. 148). It is the remnant group in this area which was the occasion for Brotherton, so we can assume that they were Unami Lenape.

By the mid-eighteenth century, however, they were referred to by the colonists as the "Cranbury Band," or "Bethel Indians," or sometimes related to the vicinity of Crosswicks (Edwards, 1822 [1749]: p. 281); Weslager, 1972: pp. 262–263), which seems to have come about as follows. Crosswicks ("*Closweeksung* or 'place of separation,'" Smith, 1765: p. 408 note n; Allinson in Barber and Howe, 1844: p. 512) was a Delaware settlement in 1692, when Anglo-Americans first arrived (Middleton, 1932). It became a small town in which the Provincial Assembly occasionally met as early as 1716, in order to avoid smallpox at nearby Burlington (Smith, 1765: p. 408). Evidently the Indian and White communities here coexisted, because there were about 150 Delaware here on March 26, 1746, when a sermon was preached to them by David Brainerd, the strongly motivated young Presbyterian missionary of the Great Awakening (Allinson, 1875: p. 36 n). A few weeks later this band moved about a dozen miles northeast "to some better lands they owned near Cranbury, that they might be more compact for worship and school, and attain better agricultural results" (Allinson, 1875: p. 36 n). In other words, this group was already acting to improve its condition in terms of the surrounding White culture—at least, as described by some White commentators. It is quite probable that the move of such a village band was also consistent with aboriginal practice, and was within the strip of land traditionally used by this band, in the narrow part of central New Jersey, where water transportation from the Delaware Valley to the Millstone and then the Raritan and the Atlantic was easy. The move which so pleased the missionary may simply have been what this group of Lenape, sometimes referred to as the Crosswicks or Cranbury band, would have done anyway when the fertility of their gardens was exhausted or one village site otherwise undesirable (Zeisberger, 1910: p. 87; Newcomb, 1956: p. 24; Weslager, 1972).

Whatever the reasons and desirability from the point of view of this band, or of David Brainerd, it was unreasonable and undesirable to some landowners near Cranbury. On the ninth of April, 1746, a John Bain made a deposition to the governor's Provincial Council, complaining that only two Indians had lived near Cranbury for the last six years, "but now some *40 Men* moved to live there," and that there was talk of three hundred more Indians coming from the Delaware. Bain said the White settlers

> there about were extremely Alarmed, at this number of Indians coming to Settle there, where its Esteemed impossible for such a Number to Live, without Stealing or killing their Neighbours' creatures (*N. J. Archives* 6: pp. 406–407).

Further, it was reported that the Indians were coming because "one Mr. Brainard" was planning to teach Christianity, and that this band would "build a Town, a Church, and a School House." The presence of these Delawares would be an added threat because there had been some "riots" among Whites in the area during the previous fall over land titles, and the rioters had then threatened to enlist the aid of Indians. Thus the move of the "Crosswicks Band" to what may well have been a traditional alternative village site near Cranbury not only posed a threat to Anglo-American farmers in the area, chiefly owing to anticipated loss of livestock, but it interfered with a land-title dispute.

David Brainerd, like some missionaries who would follow him in this calling, was evidently very sincere in his labors for the Lenape he considered his congregation, and self-sacrificing to the point of selling his own possessions to raise money for the school he hoped would aid them (D. Brainerd, 1745). He died, still a young man, in October, 1747, after having established the community, which he called "Bethel," near Cranbury (Edwards, 1822 [1749]). His younger brother, John Brainerd, then only recently graduated from Yale, took over the mission in 1748, and remained there until 1755. From 1755 until 1759 he preached in Newark, but he did not forget his mission, and evidently his labors were influential in the establishment of Brotherton in 1759, and in his own appointment as superintendent (Brainerd, 1865; Nelson, 1885, in *N.J. Archives* 9: p. 355n).

Before we analyze the creation of that reservation, however, we must examine the continuing pressures on Bethel, which was a first attempt at this sort of community. The unhappiness evident among some Whites in 1746, when this band of Delawares and David Brainerd established Bethel, continued when his brother took over. Robert Hunter Morris, one of the most extensive landholders and prominent men in New Jersey, attacked the title of the land on which the Cranbury band was settled (Nelson, 1885, in *N.J. Archives* 9: p. 355n). Other Anglo-Americans also were interested in preventing a change in the location and manner in which these Lenape lived. By the 1750's the situation was so bad that the missionary complained to the sponsoring Presbyterian agency, "the Society in Scotland for Propagating Christian

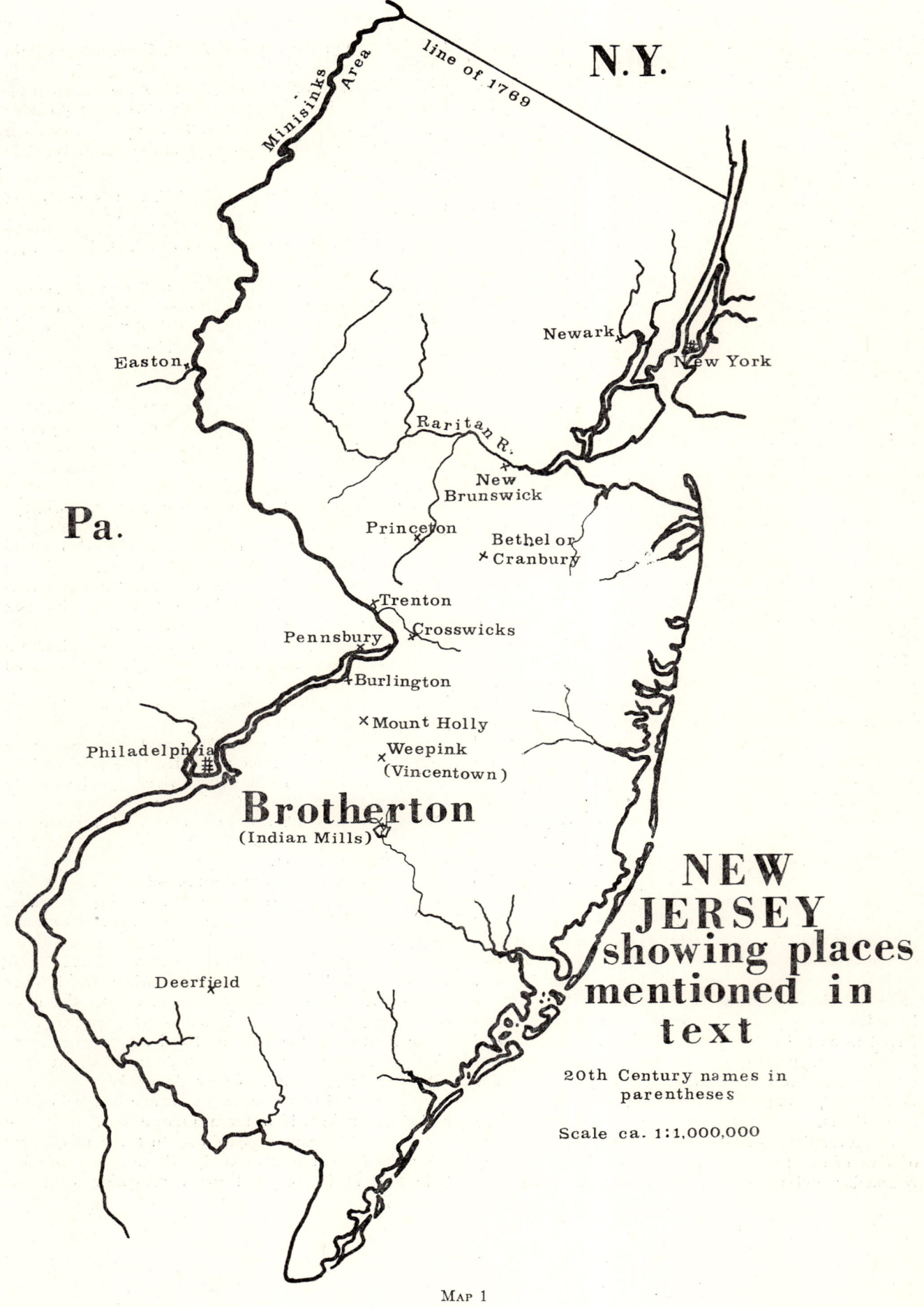

Map 1

Knowledge." At their petitioning the Lords of Trade wrote to Governor Belcher on the twenty-fifth of June, 1753, stating that John Brainerd had been "molested and obstructed in the execution of his Mission" by some colonists,

and particularly by the Indian Traders, who had persuaded the Indians that he was sent by crafty men with a view to bring them into a snare and finally deprive them of their Country and Libertys (*N. J. Archives* 8: pp. 140–141).

The governor was instructed to protect and encourage the missionary work. In 1754 the parent society in Scotland approved of an effort to buy some four thousand acres for an Indian community in New Jersey. This was apparently in response to the pressures at Bethel. The money was not appropriated, probably because of subsequent events (Nelson, 1885, in *N.J. Archives* 9: pp. 355–356n).

THE FRENCH AND INDIAN WAR

Despite this official support, John Brainerd did not stay at Bethel after 1755, but he did continue to agitate for a protected mission community for the Crosswicks-Cranbury band of Lenape. During the interval between his leaving Bethel and the creation of Brotherton a major crisis finally forced the provincial government to take action on Indian affairs. This was the outbreak of the recurrent eighteenth-century world struggle between France and England, this phase being the Seven Years War (1755–1763), the North American aspect of which was the French and Indian War. George Washington's Virginia troops triggered the events by clashing with a French scouting party in western Pennsylvania, and then surrendering to the subsequent French punitive force sent from Fort Duquesne. The following year General Braddock led a British and colonial expeditionary force to attack Fort Duquesne, but instead he gained a different sort of historical immortality, and the British regulars in North America developed a pronounced fear of being caught in a forest battle—a fear that lasted until Colonel Bouquet's victory at Bushy Run a decade later (Shy, 1965; Pargellis, 1936; Hunter, 1960; Yaple, 1968).

The French had been aided in their victory of July 9, 1755, by Indians from Canada, and few or none of the Indians resident in western Pennsylvania took part (Hunter, 1954). In the months following, however, a number of groups were persuaded to "take up the Tomahawk" against the English colonies. These included Mingo (Iroquois settled on the Ohio and its tributaries), Shawnee, and some Delawares who had moved that far west (Downes, 1940; P. A. W. Wallace, 1945; Larrabee, n.d., *b*). In the fall of 1755 small parties of these Indians, sometimes accompanied by a few French, started raiding the frontiers of Virginia, Maryland, and Pennsylvania (Hunter, 1960). No raids occurred at this time in New Jersey, but many refugees fled across the Delaware from Pennsylvania.

In the Minisink country (of which northwestern New Jersey is part) the Pennsylvania bank of the river was abandoned to the enemy, the fires from burning farms could be seen, and a few New Jersey men patrolling into Pennsylvania were killed by Indians. The reaction of the provincial government was swift, if somewhat confused. Some ten thousand New Jersey militia were called up, and temporarily marched to the exposed frontier of the province. Eventually a line of small posts, supplemented by ranging stations, were established, and a permanent force of New Jersey troops was maintained in the Minisinks until the end of hostilities in the fall of 1758 (Larrabee, 1970).

All of this was occurring far away from the densely settled part of the province, and from the village of Delaware Indians near Cranbury, but the fears of the Anglo-American population had been aroused, and the Bethel and Cranbury Indians petitioned Governor Belcher for protection. On December 3, 1755, the governor issued a proclamation requiring that each magistrate should keep a Registry book listing all Indians resident in his jurisdiction, and should issue a Certificate of Registration to each Indian, who was to keep it with him at all times, and wear a red ribbon for instant recognition as a "friendly." Any Indian not registered after twenty days was to be imprisoned until he could produce "Security for his Good Behavior" (*N.J. Archives* 16: pp. 571–573). There probably were not more than a few hundred Indians involved, and presumably only adult males were of any concern, so there may have been less than a hundred Delawares to be so registered. The very fact that such a registry certificate and badge system was ordered (I know of no evidence as to its effectiveness) suggests that the provincial government, at least, thought that these Lenape were accustomed to some of the mechanisms of European society. That such assumed acculturation was not a one-way phenomenon is shown by the stipulation in a New Jersey law passed on June 2, 1756, "for the better Regulation of the Forces upon the Frontiers" which required that "for the more effectual preventing any false alarms or mistakes when tracting the Indian Enemy . . . [no one] . . . shall wear or put on any Indian Shoes, or Maukesons" (*Session Laws* 1741–1756, Vol. II, 29 George II, 6th Session, 3rd Sitting: pp. 51, 63). Evidently not all colonists wore traditional European footgear.

Closely following the proclamation for registry, in January, 1756, a conference was held at Crosswicks. The complaints registered by the Delawares then were embodied in a law passed by the New Jersey Assembly fourteen months later. During the interim the provincial government, on June 2, 1756, joined with Pennsylvania in officially declaring war on the Shawnee and Delaware Indian Nations, and offered a scalp bounty (*N.J. Archives* 17: pp. 29–31). This led, within the month, to the murder of an Indian woman and three children in central New Jersey. The husband escaped to raise an alarm, and the White men accused of the murder were captured, tried, and executed, amid expressions of revulsion by provincial officials (*N.J. Archives* 17: pp. 38–40). By the eighteenth of July the governor suspended the aggressive policy (Huntington: LO 1317).

Finally, in March, 1757, the Assembly enacted the items of the treaty conference held in January, 1756. These items are very revealing of the conflicts between the cultures (*Session Laws* 30 George II, 7th Session, 3rd Sitting; Nevill, 1761: pp. 125–128; Allinson, 1776: pp. 212–213). Five Commissioners were appointed to deal with the Indians and to investigate land-sale grievances. Sale of liquor to Indians was severely restricted, and all land sales made or debts incurred by Indians which involved liquor were voided. The law forbade imprisonment of Indians for debt and protected their clothing and hunting equipment from seizure. Trapping of deer by non-Indians was prohibited, with a fine as penalty, or "if the Owner, or Setter of the trap shall be a Slave, he shall, in Lieu of such a Fine, be publickly whipt with Thirty Lashes, and committed till the cost is paid," and the traps were to be broken in front of a Justice of the Peace, and the parts then sold as scrap metal by the Overseer of the Poor. There are indications here of conflicts of interest involving Indian hunting rights not only as opposed to Whites, but also to Blacks.

The most important aspect of the law for intercultural relations concerned land transactions. This was specifically intended to prevent complaints regarding fraudulent land sales or leases. Before any such dealing, six Indian men were required to sign a certificate saying that the Indian or Indians claiming to own the land did so. They had to sign before a Magistrate who had to "certify that the *Indians* were Men grown, and sober, and signed in his presence." One of the high officers of the province (the governor, commander in chief of forces, one of the Council, or a justice of the Supreme Court) then had to read and explain the deed to the Indian vendor(s), and had to endorse on the back of the deed that the Indian(s) "understood the Deed or Lease, and had a reasonable Price as commonly paid on the Execution thereof," and also had to certify that he had seen all other certifications required by law. Many of the prior problems of land sales between members of the Lenape and Anglo-American societies can be read clearly in the remedies proposed here.

It is doubtful that any sales were made under these complicated conditions, because within the next year and a half a final settlement was made on all remaining land claims. In the meantime, the Presbyterian Society for the Propagation of Christian Knowledge was also active in trying to resolve the difficulties of the Delawares left in central New Jersey. The New York Correspondents worried in 1755 about the probable dispossession of the band at Bethel and urged that the society should buy land or apply to the government for a grant of land. In 1756 the Correspondents reported that they had prospects for purchasing a 3,000-acre tract in New Jersey, well adapted as a missionary community in John Brainerd's opinion, for about £450. The New York members had raised £150, and urged the parent society in Scotland to provide the balance. This the Scottish society approved in November, 1757, but the money was never sent, perhaps because of parallel action by the province. At any rate, it is clear that this sector of White culture was endeavoring to "settle" the Crosswicks-Cranbury band of Delawares on a relatively isolated and legally secure piece of land (Nelson, 1885, in *N.J. Archives* 9: pp. 356–357n). Not only the Presbyterians were active. In April, 1757, Samuel Smith, a prominent Quaker and later the author of a history of the province, drew up the constitution of the "New Jersey Association for Helping the Indians," and signed its subscription list with £20 (Smith, 1765: pp. v-vi). The first article proposed the purchase of about 2,000 acres in south central New Jersey to be held by the Association, its use to be restricted to native Indians in perpetuity, free of rent. About £175 was pledged in all (Nelson, 1885, in *N.J. Archives* 9: p. 356n).

Eventually it was neither of these sectarian moves, but an official provincial act, which established the new community. Clearly, however, considerable pressure was building from these private but concerned groups. A second conference was held at the Crosswicks site of the central New Jersey Lenape from the twenty-first to the twenty-third of February, 1758, between the governor, one Jacob Spicer, a leading Quaker in the Assembly, and the five provincial commissioners appointed in the law of the previous March, and over thirty named Indians. These included "Teedyescunk, king of the Delawares" (who had been living in the Wyoming Valley of Pennsylvania, but had land claims in central New Jersey, Wallace, 1949), one Delaware from the Susquehanna, ten from Crosswicks, two "mountain Indians" (presumably from northern New Jersey), one "Raritan Indian," three from Ancocus, twelve from Cranbury, two "southern Indians" and evidently a few others (Smith, 1765: p. 442). The results of this conference were that on the twenty-third of February, 1758, a release was signed by twenty-eight of those named, confirming that they had no further land claims in the southern half of New Jersey (usually expressed as "south of Raritan"), except for a specified list of twenty-two tracts in which particular Lenape individuals had an interest. All these tracts were in the central area of the province, in which this distinct group had been residing (Smith, 1765: pp. 443–445, Deeds *Liber* 1-2: pp. 45–47; also *Liber* 0: pp. 401–403). The deed was accompanied by a power-of-attorney by the twenty-eight Delawares to five others, all witnessed by four White citizens, and then by a Burlington County judge. These five "Indian attorneys" wrote a week later on March 8 to "Friend Mr. Israel Pemberton" in Philadelphia, asking for advice on how to seek satisfaction both for their outstanding land claims and for their desire to be securely settled (Allinson, 1875: p. 38). It may be significant that during this same period Pemberton, called "King of the Quakers" because of his leadership of the Quaker and Mennonite party in Pennsylvania politics, was involved in an effort to use the substantial Pennsylvania claims of Teedyuscung and other Delawares, including the notorious "Walking Purchase" of 1737, to embarrass the proprietary government of the Penn family (Thayer, 1943; P. A. W. Wallace, 1945; A. F. C. Wallace, 1949; Hunter, 1961).

It is not known what Pemberton's advice was, but it was undoubtedly consonant with the efforts of Samuel Smith, Jacob Spicer, and other prominent New Jersey Friends to seek a pacific solution to the "Indian War" which had plagued the middle colonies for three years now. This was evidently also the desire of the new royal governor of New Jersey, Francis Bernard, who arrived from England on June 14, 1758, to find that the worst raids of the war in the experience of New Jersey were in progress on the Minisink frontier (Larrabee, 1977). After attending to immediate problems of defense, in late June he called a general conference for all New Jersey Indians, including Teedyuscung, and the Minisink and Pompton Indians of the northern part of the colony, inviting them to Burlington, where he would "kindle a Council fire and bury all the blood that has stained our ground, deep in the Earth, and make a new chain of peace" (*N.J. Archives* 9: pp. 125–126). On August 3 the provincial Indian commissioners presented to the Assembly their report of the claims made by the Lenape at the Crosswicks Conference the previous February (N.J. Assembly Journal: pp. 319–320).

The Burlington Conference was held from August 7 through 9, and the Delawares proposed to cede all the remaining twenty-odd individual land claims in return for a secure tract of land for their community. The Indians submitted a proposal in writing, probably done by the same five "Indian Attorneys," one of whom, John Pompshire, was regularly an interpreter, and another, Stephen Calvin, was also literate in English and later was a schoolmaster at Brotherton (Allinson, 1875: pp. 40, 46). They stated that they wanted a tract called "Edge Pillock," then owned by one Benjamin Springer (Smith, 1765: p. 446; Allinson, 1875: pp. 38, 41). There had been at least one sawmill there since 1742 (*N.J. Archives* 12: p. 144), and Springer had purchased, on June 7, 1749, land from Benjamin Moore (Deeds, *Liber* G-G: p. 330), which Moore had previously taken under proprietary survey in 1710 (Surveyors General Office-Basse Book, p. 1227). The proprietors for West Jersey had included this land in larger areas purchased previously from Lenape. Thus the tract was one to which the Indians laid no residual or unsatisfied claim. It had been the undisputed holding of Anglo-American colonists for two or three generations prior to this 1758 proposal.

It is possible that this was the property referred to in 1756 as having been judged suitable for a mission community by John Brainerd (Nelson, 1883, in *N.J. Archives* 9: p. 356n; Hagerty, 1960). In any event, the Assembly, then sitting in Burlington, voted to pay the costs of the previous Crosswicks and ongoing Burlington Conferences, and of provincial participation in a forthcoming general conference to be held at Easton, Pennsylvania (N.J. Assembly Journal, 8 & 12 August, 1758: pp. 322, 337). A law was passed on August 12 "to impower certain Persons to purchase the Claims of the *Indians* to Land in this Colony" (Nevill, 1761: pp. 212–214; Allinson, 1776: pp. 220–221). This set aside £1600 New Jersey Proclamation Money to settle claims, but limited the amount for "Purchase of the Claims of the Delaware Indians, now inhabiting near *Cranbury*, and to the Southward of *Raritan* River" to not more than half of that. Since this same group desired "to have Part of the Sum allowed them laid out in Land whereon they may settle and raise their necessary Subsistence," the act moved to satisfy that, and so that "they may have always in their view a lasting Monument of the Justice and Tenderness of this Colony toward them," it approved the purchase of a tract to be chosen by the commissioners, deed to be taken in the name of the governor and commissioners and their successors and heirs, "in Trust for the life of the said *Indian* Natives who have or do reside in this Colony, South of *Raritan,* and their Successors, for ever." The Indians would not be permitted to sell or lease any of the land, and Whites could not settle or cut timber on it.

However willing the Assembly was to settle the Indian claims, it was "unwilling the Sum necessary for this Expence, should be repaid by a Tax upon the Inhabitants," who were already supporting several issues of money for expenses of defense on the frontier and for support of the New Jersey Regiment which participated in imperial offensive actions against the French in northern New York. Consequently a series of lotteries was established to raise the £1600. This may have permitted contributions from the fund already subscribed to by Samuel Smith and other New Jersey Friends, if moral doubts about gambling did not interfere. Two important additional clauses were:

6. Provided, That no Conveyance to be made as above by the Indians, shall prejudice any Right they now have to hunt on any uninclosed Lands, or fish in the Rivers and Bays of this Colony

8. . . . the Land to be purchased for the Indians. . .shall not hereafter be subject to any Tax; any Law, Usage or Custom to the contrary thereof, in any wise not withstanding.

The former of these clearly was included to meet a requirement raised by the Lenape, and the latter probably was urged by Anglo-American supporters of the project, since it agrees with the 'rent free' proposal of the 1757 New Jersey Association for Helping the Indians (Smith, 1765: pp. v-vi; Nelson, 1885, in *N.J. Archives* 9: p. 356n).

The portion of the law concerning the blanket extinguishment of all Indian land claims or titles (except those few held under English law) contained a significant departure from all previous land dealings. Up to that time the provincial royal government only governed, it did not own. All real estate in the colony which had not been purchased by settlers belonged to the two Boards of Proprietors for East and West Jersey, and it was these two bodies, "owning" the land under royal charter of 1664, who had heretofore paid any settlements made with local groups of Indians. Now, however, the urgency for settling the Indian grievances was so great, under the pressure of the war, that the Commissioners were empowered to obtain any and all Indian claims "for the Use of the Freeholders in this Colony, their Heirs and Assigns, forever." This would be done by the provincial government, for the benefit of the citizens (i.e., property owners and tax payers) of the colony, in one complete transaction, because "a strict and minute Enquiry in their [the Delawares'] several Claims, will be attended with very great Difficulty, Expence, and Delay." Thus the colony itself would now "own" whatever claims the Lenape were relinquishing in this transaction.

The intimate relationship of all this to the war effort is further shown by the fact that the £1600 made available, although ultimately to be repaid by lotteries rather than any tax, would, in the meantime, be taken from appropriations "made current for the service of the present War." In other words, it would come from the £10,000 issued by a law passed the same day "for the further Defence of the Frontier of the Colony of New Jersey" (*Session Laws* 31 George II, 9 Session, 2nd Sitting; Nevill, 1761: pp. 199–211; Allinson, 1776: pp. 219–220). Thus the Assembly clearly tied its interest in defending the frontiers to its desire, albeit not ultimately at the taxpayers' expense, to settle the grievances of the Delawares.

We shall return to the actual purchase in a moment, but first we should follow the signing and sealing of the agreements. On September 12, 1758, the five Indian attorneys executed an indenture which conveyed on behalf of the group they represented to the governor and the commissioners all remaining rights in the southern half of the colony, in exchange for the new piece of land which had already been purchased (Allinson, 1875: p. 40). All these transactions were made official at the famous Easton Conference which lasted from October 8 through 26, 1758. The purpose was a general peace settlement between the imperial government and its colonies on one hand and the disaffected Indians of western Pennsylvania and the Ohio country (Smith, 1765: pp. 455–483; A. F. C. Wallace, 1949). The important part of the settlement for this study is the final ratification of the cession of all Indian land claims in New Jersey. The previously mentioned indenture of September 12 was confirmed in a memorandum written on its back at Easton on October 24 signed by Teedyuscung and other Delaware leaders, and, significantly, by several Iroquois spokesmen (Allinson, 1875: p. 40). There was considerable discussion prior to the settlement of the Indian claims to the northern part of the province, and the desires expressed there are important in establishing some of the themes persistently appearing in relations between the cultures. For example, Thomas King, an Oneida chief, representing Mohawk warriors, spoke on October 18 to Governor Bernard on behalf of the Minisinks.

You deal hardly with us; you claim all the wild creatures, and will not let us come on your land to hunt after them. You will not so much as let us peel a single tree: This is hard, and has given us great offence. The cattle you raise are your own, but those which are wild, are still ours, or should be common to both; for when we sold the land, we did not propose to deprive ourselves of hunting the wild deer, or using a stick of wood when we should have occasion. We desire the governor to take this matter into his care, and see that justice be done in it. *two strings of white wampum* (Smith, 1765: p. 470).

And again, Egohohowen, a Minisink leader, replied on October 21 to an admonition by the influential Seneca Chief Tagashata (and through him spoke to the New Jersey colonial governor and delegates):

. . . we desire, that if we should come into your province to see our old friends, and should have occasion for the bark of a tree to cover a cabin, or a little refreshment, that we be not denied, but treated as brethren: and that your people may not look on the wild beasts of the forest, or fish of the waters, as their sole property; but that we may be admitted to an equal use of them. (Smith, 1765: p. 474).

It is clear that the Indian speakers were expressing the importance to their people of free use of the renewable resources of the environment, not only the hunting and fishing needs of the men, but the figurative "stick of wood" or "bark of a tree" which represented the boreal resources utilized by both men and women. It is also clear that it is precisely this difference of view concerning the "wild" cattle (I suspect the original word may have been a more general reference to herbivores) which occasioned the memorial in 1746 when the White residents near Cranbury felt that no large body of Indians could live near them "without Stealing or killing their Neighbours' creatures" (*N.J. Archives* 6: pp. 406–407).

Finally on October 23 the "Munsies" and "Opings or Pomptons" did "Grant, Bargain and Sale release Convey and Confirm" to the governor and commissioners their interest in the northern part of the colony, for "One Thousand Spanish pieces of Eight" later in the document recipted as £375. (Deeds, *Liber* O: pp. 464–469). The southwestern boundary line of this grant was made coincident with the northeastern boundary "of the Land lately Granted and released by the Delaware Indians ... the 12th Day of September," and each group confirmed the grant of the other, so that in this final grand release the cessions of Lenape land claims in the northern and southern halves of the colony were made interlocking. This release also included "all the woods, Waters and all the privileges and advantages thereto belonging or in any wise appertaining Exept: any right they now have to hunt in any uninclosed lands or fish in the Rivers and Bays of this Colony." It would appear that the "collecting" rights to "a stick of wood" were overlooked or ignored. Various witnesses signed, initialed, or marked this release and appended memoranda, such as George Croghan, who was at this time Sir William Johnson's deputy agent for Indian affairs in the northern colonies (Volweiler, 1926), Henry Montur, "King's Interpreter," Conrad Weiser "provincial Interpreter for Pennsylvania" who was now losing his influence and was only, as a Mohawk said, "a fallen tree" (*Pennsylvania Colonial Record* 9: p. 491; P. A. W. Wallace, 1945), the Oneida Thomas King, the Seneca Tagashata, the Cayuga Tohahoyo, "Egohohoun, Chief of the Minisinks," and a number of "Oping or Pompton" or "Wappingers," and several of the central Jersey Lenape such as Stephen Calvin and Moses "Tattamy." After all this it was with great satisfaction that Governor Bernard reported to the Lords of Trade on October 31 that "by the mediation of some of the Chiefs of the United Nations" he had reached agreement with the "Minissinks &c & have paid them 1000 dollars" for "all their claims to the Province of New Jersey." Both this and the earlier release of the southern part had been witnessed by Iroquois chiefs and had been made known to all nearby Indian groups "as a full acquittal and discharge of all Indian claims upon the province of New Jersey: and the United Nations have received from me a large belt as a perpetual Memorial of this transaction" (*N.J. Archives* 9: p. 141).

THE CREATION AND MAINTENANCE OF BROTHERTON

There remained now the problem of settling the Cranbury-Crosswicks band of Lenape in their new community. In the same letter of October 31, 1758, the governor wrote that

a tract containing 3,000 Acres has been purchased ... and Notice has been given that all Indians that propose to reside in this Province (which according to an exact return made to me are now about 270) must resort to that tract of land which is extremely convenient for their purpose having a large Wast adjoining to it for their hunting and a passage to the Sea for fishing: And we are going to build a Town for them, there being a Saw Mill allready there & a grist Mill is immediately to be erected. This place is in the County of Burlington & adjoining to the barren Pine Land & out of the Way of Communication with the wilder Indians. Thus has the Southern claim been settled to the best advantage of both parties (*N. J. Archives* 9: p. 140-141).

Governor Bernard *expected* the Delawares to continue hunting and fishing *outside* the tract, in the unoccupied, and at that time undesirable, pine barrens (the large area of the Wharton State Forest now borders three sides of this land). A town and mills would be provided, but the continuation of pre-contact Indian subsistence was also anticipated. In fact, a nineteenth-century description of the use of the area by the Delawares who moved there after 1758 states that "the rights of fishing and hunting as secured by the treaty were freely used, and also the traditionary right of felling timber and cutting basket stuff, mentioned in the conferences, but not referred to in the written agreements" (Allinson, 1875: p. 46). Also evident is the governor's desire to isolate this band from "the wilder Indians," which seems to have also been desired by these particular Delawares themselves.

The tract had been purchased on the twenty-ninth of August, and the deed recorded by the provincial secretary on September 7, 1758 (Deeds, *Liber* O: pp. 394–400). Since these events were only three and four weeks after the Lenape had stated, at Burlington, their interest in this land, the business seems to have been concluded with considerable speed. This may have been because of the desire of the provincial Indian commissioners to settle matters before the upcoming Easton Conference, because the February cession deed to all southern New Jersey except certain tracts was confirmed and recorded at the same time as the purchase (Deeds, *Liber* O: pp. 401–403, entry of same day immediately following the Springer deed) and because on September 12 the five Indian attorneys—on behalf of the Crosswicks-Cranbury band—ceded the remaining specific tracts in exchange for the Edge-Pillock property as a secure home. However, the speed with which the business was completed also suggests prior contacts and agreements. Very likely this property had been selected earlier, perhaps as early as 1756 by John Brainerd.

The price of the purchase was £740 paid to Springer and £5 more to his wife for her Dower Right. All previous sales of the tract are included in the deed, to clear title, and the land had been surveyed for this sale. The several pieces Springer owned totaled 1,983 acres by their original measure, but the new survey showed the actual acreage to be 3,044. Included were "the houses, Mills buildings, Orchards Fences and improvem'ts" (397), or "Houses Mills Buildings and premises" (397), or "the Saw Mill, Houses Lands and premises" (399). The map of the survey accompanying the recorded deed shows an "Old Mill," a "New Mill," and "Springer's House," shown as two stories (400). Thus the deed is ambiguous regarding improvements. There was certainly a fairly substantial farm house, and at least one mill, evidently a sawmill. There may have been another mill, and probably there

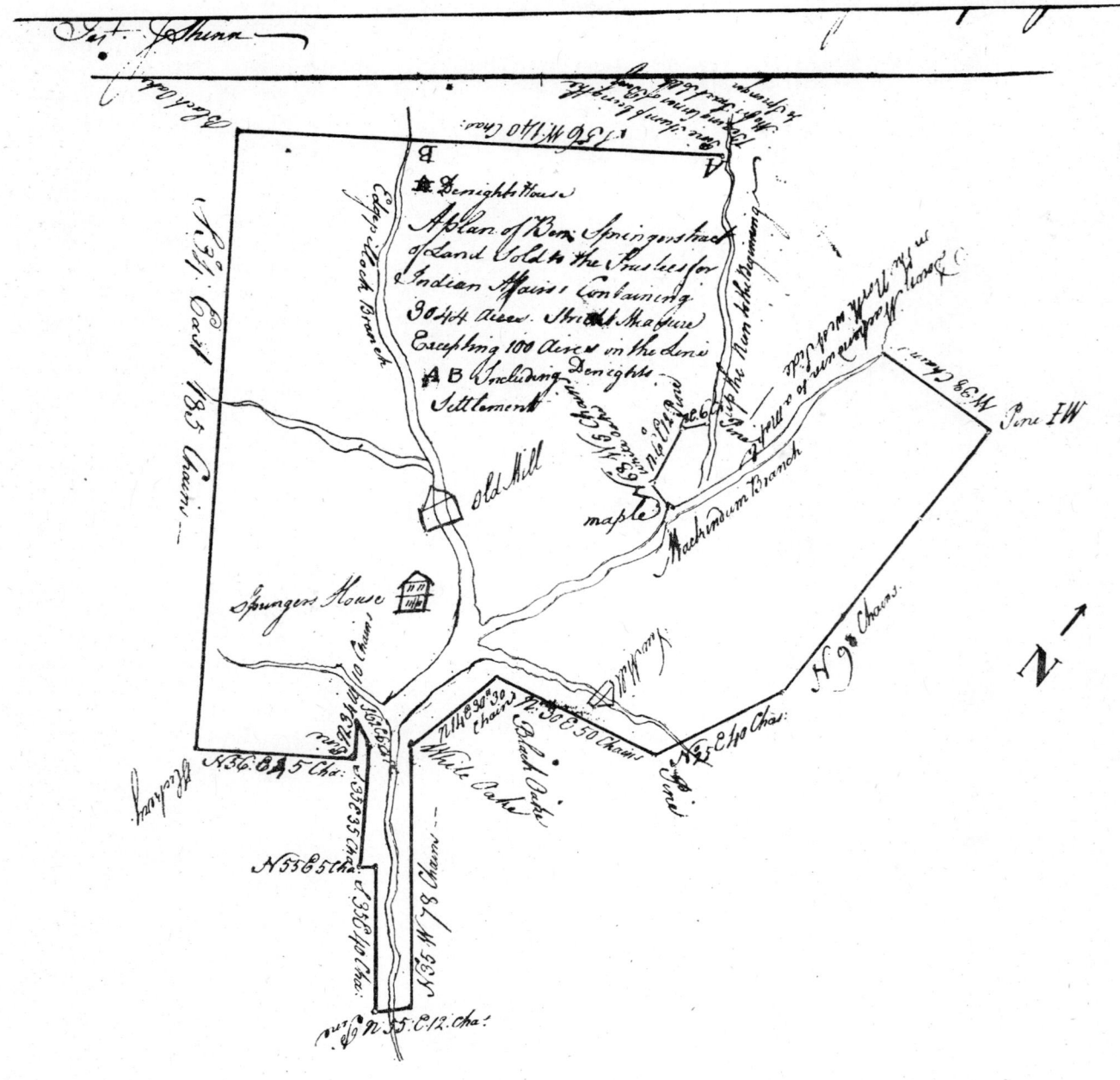

Map 2. Survey of the "Edgepillock" (later, "Brotherton") tract in 1758, accompanying the Benjamin Springer deed to New Jersey. This was purchased 29 August and recorded 7 September, 1758 (Deeds, Liber O: p. 400).

was some fencing, orchards, and cleared ground. In his letter of October 31 the governor said there was "a Saw Mill allready there & a grist Mill is immediately to be errected" (*N.J. Archives* 9: p. 141), which suggests that the word "Mills" in the deed may be overly general, and one of the mills on the map may have been only a site, disused or only proposed.

Some of the Delawares must have moved to the new location within the following seven months, because on June 15, 1759, Governor Bernard reported that in the two weeks previous he went to Burlington County to lay out the Indian Town there.... the Indians were removed to the place: It is a tract of Land Very suitable for this purpose, having soil good enough, a large hunting country and a passage by water to the Sea for fishing ... & has a saw mill upon it which serves to provide them with timber for their own use & to raise a little money for other purposes. To this place I went with 3 of the Commissioners for Indian affairs, where we laid out the plan of a town, to which I gave the Name of Brotherton & saw an house erected being one of ten that were ready prepared; & afterwards ordered lots of land to be laid out for the Indians to clear & till, the land allready cleared being to remain in common till they have acquired themselves separate property, by their own industry. We also made an appointment of an house & lands for a Minister, I having engaged Mr. Brainerd a Scotch presbyterian for that purpose, for which he is most peculiarly suited. The next day I had a conference with the chiefs, at which they expressed great satisfaction at what had been done for them, & I assured them that the same care of them should be continued & exhorted them to order, sobriety & industry. The whole Number of them at present does not amount to 200, & when We have gathered together all in the province they will not be 300. If I can but keep them from being supplied with rum, for which there are laws strict enough, I shall hope to make them orderly & useful Subjects (*N. J. Archives* 9: pp. 174–175).

The governor again repeated the desirability of keeping this group out of communication with Indians on the frontier.

Here are expressed many plans and objectives to which we shall refer later, such as the temporary use of cleared land in common, pending the Delaware's "earning" of their own, individually occupied, fields, through labor, or the hope of turning members of another culture into "orderly & useful Subjects" of the crown. For the moment the important points are that a majority of the approximately 270 Lenape of central New Jersey, loosely referred to as the Crosswicks-Cranbury band, were now at Brotherton, and John Brainerd had an official appointment as resident missionary. A "town" was "laid out," probably as a village along a street in eighteenth-century New Jersey colonial fashion, and ten houses were in some way "ready prepared." Since the sawmill (evidently the only mill) was working, we can guess that lumber was being cut there, and that these houses were frame structures covered with weather boarding, of Anglo-American style. The governor saw one house erected, and it is likely, but not certain, that the other nine also were put up shortly thereafter.

From later evidence, it seems that Brainerd's residence was in the general location where the Springers' house stood, so in all likelihood the one fairly substantial residence already there was assigned to this resident White protector and guide. Other sources report that soon after this a "meeting-house was built of logs" (Allinson, 1875: p. 46). Brotherton is close to the lower Delaware portion of New Jersey where what we now think of as traditional frontier log buildings were introduced by Swedish immigrants in the mid-seventeenth century. Here the style persisted until its popularity suddenly increased greatly on the mid-eighteenth-century frontier (Mercer, 1924; Shurtleff, 1939). This church in question apparently stood until about 1808, when it was burned (Barber and Howe, 1844: p. 121).

A school was established, probably using the meeting house. "Stephen Calvin, an interpreter at the Crosswicks and Easton treaties, was a schoolmaster" (Allinson, 1875: p. 46). Later Stephen's son Bartholemew Calvin, who studied at the College of New Jersey (now Princeton University), also taught at the Brotherton school, "and had as many White as Indian scholars." The lawyer Samuel Allinson who published a compendium of New Jersey Laws in 1776 "frequently visited the settlement," thought Bartholemew Calvin was a good teacher, and collected money for books for the school (Allinson, 1875: p. 46).

As late as two years after the establishment of Brotherton, part of the earlier residence pattern persisted. In August, 1761, Brainerd wrote that there were "something upward of an hundred old and young" there, a "small settlement perhaps near forty" a dozen miles away (presumably the Weepink community), some seventeen miles further (Cranbury) was a third group about the same size, and "yet some few scattering ones still about Crossweeksung." The total, said Brainerd, might be two hundred (DeCou, 1932).

Not all the promised support from the provincial government was forthcoming. Brainerd appealed to the Assembly in 1761 for aid in erecting a school, gristmill, blacksmithy, and trading store, "but the Quaker influence in the Assembly defeated the project" (Nelson, 1885, in *N.J. Archives* 9: pp. 356–357, note). In addition to this note of White sectarian competition, simple unwillingness to spend public money is very likely. Whether the province actually paid Brainerd is unknown. On May 19, 1759, he signed a receipt to the "Treasurer of the College of New Jersey" for £8 which Brainerd had paid the "Indian School-Master" (presumably one of the Calvins), and £10 "in part of my salary for the ensuing year on Acct of the Indian Mission I have undertaken." Again on May 31, 1764, he signed for £18, "being the interest for one year of the money at the disposal of the Synod for Indian Missions." The receipt of June 9, 1767, refers to the £18 as interest on £300 managed by the Synod of New York and Philadelphia and "incorporated in the College Fund." Further receipts on the seventh of April, 1769, and the fifth of April, 1770, also state that the £18 interest (6 percent on the £300 fund) was "for Indian Affairs" and "for the Support of a Missionary among the Indians" (John Brainerd papers). It seems certain then that at least some of Brainerd's support was coming from a Presbyterian Indian mission fund being managed by the College of New Jersey, of which, incidentally, Brainerd was a trustee.

There is an official commission from Governor Josiah Hardy, who succeeded Governor Boone over a year after the departure of Bernard, appointing John Brainerd in charge of the Indians at Brotherton on March 22, 1762 (Deeds, *Liber* AAA: p. 369; *N.J. Archives* 9: pp. 355–358). Either the previous administration had failed to make Brainerd's appointment official, or a new document was felt necessary with a new governor. The stated reasons were both "for the Service of the said Indians as for the Quiet of the Inhabitants being near ... Brotherton, that some Person should be Appointed to take care of and Superintend such Indians," so Brainerd was appointed "Superintendent and Guardian of the said Indians and every of them, and of ... Brotherton." Perhaps it was mostly to satisfy the worries of nearby Whites that Brainerd's status was raised from mere missionary to being effectively legal guardian of the tract and the Delawares on it.

A fragment of John Brainerd's journal exists, from January, 1761, to October, 1762 (J. Brainerd, 1761–1762; Jonathan Brainerd, 1880). Here are described his varied efforts to proseletyze, including preaching in several Anglo-American towns in central New Jersey, and occasional other business such as trustees' meetings at Princeton. The church emphasis is probably a result of this journal being a report to supporters in Scotland (Jonathan Brainerd, 1880: p. 2). References to his Lenape congregation, other than as an audience for his lessons, are tantalizingly few. On the week of March 1 through 7, 1761, he "spent some time ... with the Indians about their Temporal Business; Particular with Regard to preparing their ground for corn and other seed" (J. Brainerd, 1761–1762: pp. 6–7). In mid-July he spent part of a week "visiting the Indians at their respective Habitations" (J. Brainerd, 1761–1762: p. 17). This may have included not only their residences at Brotherton, but also a nearby small group residing "off reservation" at "Weepink," about ten miles north of Brotherton near the present Vincentown (Jonathan Brainerd, 1880: pp. 23–25), where he raised money for a joint Indian-White church on March 9, 1762 (J. Brainerd, 1761–1762: p. 32). He visited another small Indian settlement near Pennsbury, on the Pennsylvania side of the Delaware River (30 August & 4 October, 1761, J. Brainerd, 1761–1762: pp. 19, 20–21). In March, 1762, Brainerd recorded spending several evenings with the Indians "contriving about temporal Affairs; viz. mending of Bridges, fencing of Land, getting ready for Planting, & the like" and a week later assisted them in doing some of these (J. Brainerd, 1761–1762: pp. 32, 33). In April he tried to keep a group who were clearing land from having "too much Strong Drink," and settled differences between a married couple (J. Brainerd, 1761–1762: p. 36). An area of problems seems to have been cutting of Indian timber by Whites, and Brainerd spent several days looking into this and consulting "the Law respecting Indian Lands at Weepink" (19 April & 23 April, J. Brainerd, 1761–1762: pp. 37, 38). It is possible that all these problems were at Weepink, rather than at Brotherton. The missionary felt it worthy of note when, during "Forenoon Exercises, one of the Indians (a professor) who had been unhappily overtaken with Drunkeness, made a very penitent confession & promised Reformation" (24 June, J. Brainerd, 1761–1762: p. 45). Besides alcohol, absenteeism seems to have been an occasional difficulty, as when Brainerd had to omit a Sunday evening sermon because of "the Indians having been much abroad of late, providing Fodder against winter &c" (1 Aug., 1762, J. Brainerd, 1761–1762: p. 49). I suspect that the Lenape were as much adhering to their earlier pattern of summer foraging as to a new pattern of collecting "Fodder," which we may presume was for livestock although there is no other evidence regarding ownership of animals by the Brotherton Delawares.

During the period covered by these journals, but not recorded by Brainerd, the mill burned. On September 22, 1762, the "Indians settled at *Brotherton*" petitioned the Assembly, saying

that their Provision, Clothing and Nails, for building, the first Year they came to *Brotherton,* amounted to about £106; which they are still in Debt for; and that their Mill is lately burnt which renders them utterly unable to pay their said Debt; and praying, that the Province will pay the same; as they have had some Reason to expect: (N. J. Assembly Journal—Votes 1755–1767—No. 61: p. 15).

Evidently the sawmill had been a small source of income, as Governor Bernard had hoped, and its loss was felt. The debt for nails supports the supposition that at least the ten houses were erected, and that they were of frame construction. The Brotherton Delawares undoubtedly referred to Governor Bernard's speech to them in early June, 1759, when he "assured them that the same care of them should be continued" (*N.J. Archives* 9: p. 175). The legislature was of a different mind, and the petition was referred to the next session, and never taken up.

From this point on, the Brotherton community seems to have declined in number, and probably in morale. Writing in 1765 the historian Samuel Smith said that the Indians "remained to their satisfaction" at Brotherton, "having their usual means of living very convenient," but he numbered them at only "about sixty persons," with twenty more "at Weekpink, on a tract formerly secured by an English right, to the family of king Charles, an Indian Sachem" (1765: pp. 483–484). Pontiac's rebellion brought a return of New Jersey militia to the Minisink front (N.J. Assembly Journal, p. 171, Vote of 22 November, 1763), but no new interest in relations with the resident Lenape. In 1768 Governor Franklin and Chief Justice Smith attended the treaty conference at Fort Stanwix, New York, but evidently took no special interest in Brotherton. In the same year John Brainerd moved to Mount Holly, but returned to preach at Brotherton (Nelson, 1885, in *N.J. Archives* 9: p. 355). He seems to have resided at Brotherton again from 1775 to 1777 and then moved to Deerfield in southern New Jersey where he died in 1781. We have seen that he continued to receive pay for his missionary efforts at least until 1770, and he obtained admission to the College of New Jersey for Bartholemew Calvin, but I suspect Brainerd was losing interest in his efforts at religious conversion and cultural transformation. The situation was considered

TABLE 1
Estimated Lenape Community Population in Central New Jersey from 1746 to 1802

Date	Source	Cranbury	Crosswicks	All others	Weepink	Brotherton	Total
1746	Bain Deposition	"40 men" (total probably about 100)	(some)	—	—	0	—
Feb. 1758	Representation at Crosswick Conference	12	9	5	4 (As "Ancocous & Southern")	0	31 (men)
Oct. 1758	Governor Bernard	—	—	—	—	0	270
June 1759	Governor Bernard					Less than 200	Less than 300
Aug. 1761	Brainerd	About 40	A few	—	About 40	More than 100	About 200
1765	Smith	—	—	—	20	About 60	—
1774	Governor Franklin	—	—	—	—	50–60	50–60
1802	Report to Governor	—	—	—	—	63 adults had rights (total over 100?)	—
1802	Allinson	—	—	—	—	70–80 were removed	

bad enough in November, 1771, so that the Brotherton band petitioned Governor Franklin to lease some of their land to Anglo-American farmers, but the Provincial Assembly felt this would lead to alienation of the Indian possession, so the request was denied (N.J. Assembly Journal, pp. 308, 309). Besides, it was specifically prohibited in the third clause of the Act of August 12, 1758, which authorized the creation of this protected community. Governor Franklin counted the population of Indians at Brotherton as fifty to sixty in 1774 (*N.J. Archives* 10: p. 447). John Hunt, a Quaker preacher, in January, 1777, visited "the poor Indians at Edgepelick and found them in very low circumstances as to food and raiment" (DeCou, 1932).

A summary of the estimated number of Delawares may be of interest, although it will reveal, as much as anything, the difficulty that Anglo-American colonists had in making a census of Indians. This suggests that the band that moved from Crosswicks to Cranbury in 1746 numbered about one hundred or a little more, and that approximately this same number moved to Brotherton, which had between one and two hundred during the first few years, but later declined to less than half that. It seems to have taken several years for remnant families to leave the old sites at Cranbury and Crosswicks (which were about equally represented at the February, 1758, conference). What is not clear is whether members of outlying Delaware settlements moved into Brotherton, even while the overall population shrank, or whether they moved out of the province, died, or simply ceased to be counted as Indians. If any one of the latter three possibilities is true, then it would seem that the community at Brotherton suffered a severe reduction in population between 1761 and 1765, possibly after the disappointment of receiving no further government support following the mill fire and subsequent petition. Population then was relatively stable for a decade, and probably for a full generation, if the figures for removal, in the following section of this paper, are correct. Weslager records abortive attempts to sell Brotherton and move west between 1767 and 1771 (1972: pp. 271–273).

Whatever the size of the community, it was felt to be in economic trouble. On February 17, 1796, a petition was placed before the state legislature on "behalf of the Indian Natives residing at Brotherton" requesting an alteration in the 1758 Act, and the appointment of new Commissioners "to take charge of the Lands and Mill at Brotherton, and let or lease the same for the Use and Benefit of the Indians" (N.J. Assembly Journal—Votes 1793–1796: Session 27 October, 1795: p. 18). Three days later the Assembly Journal records that a report was received from committee urging approval of such action, "in Order to effectuate the Benevolent Object of the Government in making said purchase" (pp. 24–25). The bill was debated on March 10 and passed unanimously on the fifteenth (pp. 51, 58). The two Whites who presented the petition, and another man, were commissioned to lease the land in a way beneficial to the Indians, and to pay the rent, "or the value in necessaries, to those most needing aid" (Allinson, 1875: p. 47). The scene was now set for the final termination of this eighteenth-century attempt to create a reservation whereon Indians could become "orderly & useful" citizens of Anglo-American society.

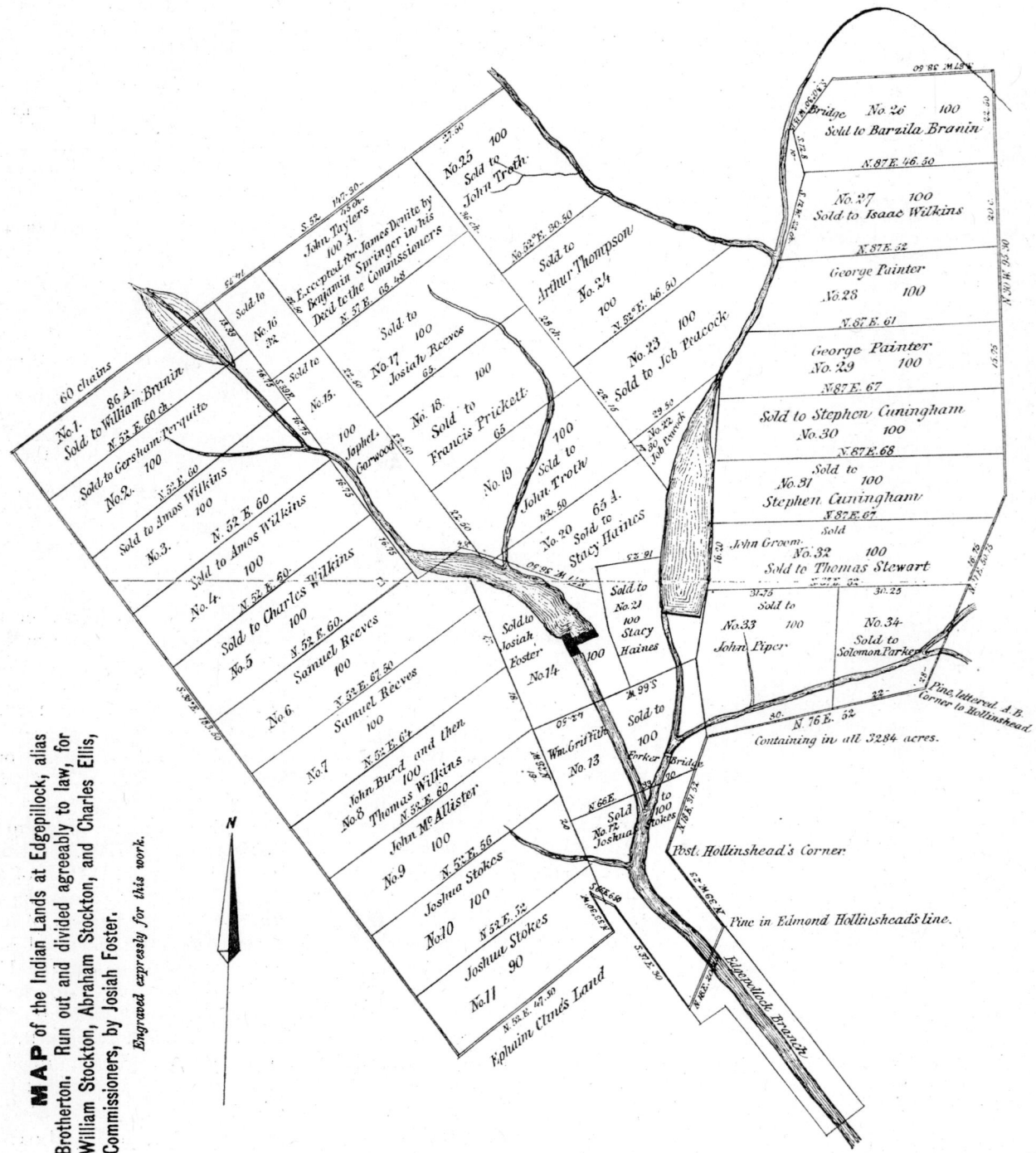

MAP 3. A map of the 1802 property division at the sale of Brotherton to various purchasers. This engraved copy was published by Woodward and Hageman (1883: p. 414a).

LIQUIDATION OF THE COMMUNITY

No record was found of how the leasing operation worked, or what the Brotherton band of Delawares received. Whatever it was, it was not an overwhelming inducement to remain at the site. The Mauhkennuks, a Delawaran-speaking group resident at New Stock-bridge, N.Y., near Oneida Lake, sent a letter to their "grandfather," the Brotherton Lenape, in 1801 inviting the latter to move in with them and "eat out of their dish" (Allinson, 1875: p. 47). An application to the state legislature followed, requesting permission to sell the land, and on December 3, 1801, a bill was passed by

24 yeas to 11 nays, authorizing the appointment of yet more Commissioners, and the sale of land in 100-acre tracts, "and to appropriate the monies thence arising for the benefit of said Indians" (N.J. Assembly Votes, p. 516). The law required that three-fourths of the adult Indians must consent to this. On January 15 two representatives of the governor met at Brotherton with the Delawares, and reported on March 20 that 38 out of 63 adults who had rights in the tract had signed their approval of sale, and 8 more had signed in Trenton on March 20. This totals 46, which is 2 adults short of the required three-fourths of 63. However, the representatives said that the necessary proportion had been met, and Governor Bloomfield accepted the report with this logic (Allinson, 1875: pp. 47–48). He appointed Commissioners on March 29, and on April 13, 1802, they ran an advertisement in the *Trenton Federalist* (p. 4, col. 1). The benefits proclaimed were numerous. "A great part of the land" was timbered with valuable trees, there was "a good saw mill in good repair" and another good location "where a mill has formerly been." Several farms were "cleared" which were "chiefly fenced with cedar rails," and there were apple orchards, other fruit trees, and "a number of houses." Sales were to begin on May 10. The land broken into 34 numbered lots, a few of less than 100 acres, and some of the buyers evidently bought more than one lot (Woodward and Hageman, 1883: p. 414a). The map of the division shows one mill and the pond where another had been. Subsequently the name "Brotherton" was lost, and by 1870 the place was called by its present name, Indian Mills (Bisbee, 1971: p. 115).

It is reported that between seventy and eighty "Indians moved to New Stockbridge accompanied by the Commissioners, who paid the removal expenses out of the sale proceeds, contributed to the New Stockbridge treasury, and invested the remainder in United States notes" (Allinson, 1875: p. 48). Another tradition reports that twelve wagons carried the infirm and belongings, and that a few Indians remained (Barber and Howe, 1844: p. 121; DeCou, 1932). The latter would seem likely, for if there were 63 adults we could expect a total population of at least 100, probably more, depending on the age distribution. It is noteworthy that these numbers are within the range of the size of the Brotherton community during most of its existence, and of the Bethel group at Cranbury which seems to have formed the core of those founding Brotherton.

After 1802 there were no recognized groups of Indians in New Jersey, although it is clear that some families or individuals remained, and have left descendants (DeCou, 1932; Weslager, 1972: pp. 274–281). But if the Lenape as such were gone, their relationship was not yet ended. Two decades later the Brotherton Delawares and their New Stockbridge hosts decided to leave New York State, and to purchase from the Menominee land between Winnebago Lake and Lake Michigan. Accordingly Bartholemew Calvin, the former Brotherton schoolmaster, petitioned the New Jersey legislature. Acts of November 28, 1822, and December 23, 1823, authorized the release of first $1,000 and then the balance of the fund of $3,551.23 held in trust after the sale of Brotherton, to enable the Delawares to purchase this western land (Allinson, 1875: p. 48n).

This accounted for the funds, but even so did not end the felt obligation. Another decade later the seventy-six-year-old Bartholemew Calvin once again, for the last time, presented a plea from the Delawares to the government of New Jersey. There were now some forty descendants of the Brotherton band living with the Stockbridge Indians in the community called "Statesburgh," bought from the Menominee. As they were in need, they petitioned to sell their hunting and fishing rights, which they had reserved in the treaties of 1758 and had not relinquished in giving up Brotherton in 1801–1802. Calvin stated that the rights "were once of great value to us, and we apprehend that neither time nor distance, nor the non-use of our rights, has at all affected them." The Delawares felt the state was the proper purchaser, and "humbly" prayed that the legislature would "look upon us with that eye of pity, as we have reason to think our poor untutored forefathers looked upon yours, when they first arrived ... and sold them their lands ... for trifles" (Barber and Howe, 1844: pp. 510–511). A committee of the legislature reported favorably, swayed by the oratory of Samuel L. Southard, who proclaimed, "That it was a proud fact in the history of New Jersey, that every foot of her soil has been obtained from the Indians by fair and voluntary purchase and transfer" (Barber and Howe, 1844: p. 511). Calvin asked for and received $2,000 by vote of March 12, 1832. Writing shortly afterward, one New Jersey historian expressed some legal doubts. "Considering the nature of the claims, it must be regarded as an act of beneficence as much as of justice" and "claims deemed by many imaginary, have been listened to with respectful attention" (W. J. Allinson in: Barber and Howe, 1844: p. 511). Calvin himself wrote a letter of thanks to the state legislature, saying that

The final act of official intercourse between the State of New Jersey and the Delaware Indians, who once owned nearly the whole of its territory, has now been consummated, and in a manner which must redound to the honor of this growing state, and, in all probability, to the prolongation of the existence of a wasted, yet grateful people....
Nothing save benisons can fall upon [New Jersey] from the lips of a Lenni Lenape ...(Barber and Howe, 1844: p. 511).

When this letter was read to the legislature, it was met "with shouts of acclamation." Presumably this was the elation of a "clear conscience" which came at having done an "honorable" thing. I should note that as far as can be determined, the similar hunting and fishing rights held by the Munsi and other northern New Jersey Delawaran speakers under the Easton treaty of October 23, 1758 (Deeds, *Liber* O: p. 466 bottom), has never been extinguished, and may still stand.

In the 1870's the historian Samuel Allinson asked New Jersey's Senator F. T. Freylinghuysen to inquire into the further fate of the remnant of the Brotherton band. At the Senator's request U.S. Commissioner of Indian Affairs Edward P. Smith reported that they had combined with "the Stockbridges and Munsees," and moved west of the Mississippi in 1840. A few might be "with the Stockbridges in Shawano County, Wisconsin, or with the Munsee or Chippewas in Franklin County, Kansas" (N.J. Historical Society, Newark, quoted in: Allinson, 1875: pp. 48–49n). Newcomb, tracing Delaware migrations, refers to the Stockbridge as having been "Mohican Housatonic of Massachusetts," who moved to Oneida country after 1780, and in 1832, with some Oneida and some "Christianized Munsi" to a reserve near Lake Winnebago (1956: p. 99). In 1839 about 400 moved as a group to Kansas, and settled on Delaware lands (Foreman, 1946: pp. 337–338). By 1860 they had confederated with some Chippewa in Kansas, and after the Civil War they were taken into the Cherokee Nation. Newcomb found in the early 1950's "only one person who claimed to be a Stockbridge Indian living among the 'Cherokee-Delawares'" (1956: p. 99); Weslager reports extensively on the modern Delaware, and says some "Sand Hill Delaware" still lived near the coast of New Jersey in the 1950's (1972: pp. 277–281).

III. RELEVANT THEMES

It is not practical within the limits of this paper to attempt a complete thematic analysis in Opler's sense (1945, 1946, 1949, 1959, 1968), of either Delaware or Anglo-American culture. All that is necessary for our purposes is to identify certain themes within each culture which are pertinent to our understanding of the relationship between them. From this, I hope to demonstrate that there are also themes, or similar phenomena, in the long set of dealings which we, from our cultural point of view, call "Indian Relations." Perhaps it would be better, to avoid confusion with terminology like Opler's, to speak of "continuities," or "persistences" (although this might conflict with Spicer's usage in "Persistent Cultural Systems," 1971). They are the parallels to which I alluded in the introduction, and will return after examining the relevant themes in Lenape and Anglo-American cultures. The diagram "Themal Interaction" at the end of Chapter IV illustrates the relationships discussed below.

THEMES IN DELAWARE CULTURE

1. The most important theme or emphasis affecting the relationship of the Lenni Lenape with the growing colonial population is one derived from the economic dependence of the Delawares on a subsistence supported by male hunting, general fishing, and female gardening and gathering activities. As in many such Horticultural/Hunting-and-Gathering cultural ecological systems, the primary caloric reliance was almost certainly on vegetal matter grown or gathered by the women, but the highest value was placed on protein food which men brought back from hunting the territory traditionally available to them (Chagnon, 1968; Lee and DeVore, 1968; Service, 1971; Steward, 1955). The Delawares' subsistence was what we might term "proto-horticultural," but their relative valuation of food was more that of "intensified foraging," if such a generalization is possible. The theme, then, might be expressed as: "Hunting is a more important activity than gardening or gathering, the food so produced is more valuable, and men (partly because they hunt deer, etc.), are more important in most social matters than women, who only grow corn, beans & squash, pick berries, and collect shell fish, etc." There is, of course, some limit to this emphasis, and it comes with the recognition that the vegetable matter is essential, even if not as desirable as meat, and that women produce this. A further limit would be the probable Delaware matrilineal uxorilocal residence pattern and the possible female role in choosing kin-group leaders (Newcomb, 1956; A.F.C. Wallace, 1947; Weslager, 1944; 1972).

There are several themes (or, perhaps more accurately sub-themes) which are so closely related that we might almost say that they follow from the first postulate. One of these is that there is a territory which traditionally is used by a matrilineally related kin group. Seasonal moves within this territory were necessary for the Lenape to utilize the various natural resources at the same time that they were planting and returning to harvest and store garden produce. Moreover, it was occasionally desirable to move the base of operations (i.e., the village) of the kin-related band, but probably normally within the general territory and frequently to another traditional site because of exhausted soil fertility, changes in resources, or even sanitation (Newcomb, 1956). This might be stated: "a band lives in a village, seasonally hunts and gathers a territory around this, and may have several alternate village sites." Another important value determinant which follows is that "the people of this related group share together equally in access to the resources of the territory." Finally, it is important that the animals a man finds while hunting in this territory are all potential game simply through the fact of his finding them in the territory in which he has rights to hunt. The animals, of course, do not "belong" to him, but they are all available to him for hunting. If he is successful, the resultant meat does belong to him, or to his wife to distribute, or to some other claimants if they have such rights. To a lesser degree, the same is true of the resources of an area available to gathering by women. This theme could be phrased, in Anglo-American concepts, to the effect that: "A member of a band does not 'own' (in a European's sense) a territory or the resources in it, but any appropriate animal or plant within the territory used by the band may be taken, if found."

2. A second major Delawaran theme concerns the attitude toward European culture, at least during the latter part of the seventeenth and most of the eighteenth century. This is largely reflected in material goods. Many of the specific objects which once were aboriginally produced were now replaced by White manufactured goods, although major categories were not yet changed. Examples would be the frequent use of firearms, of iron kettles for cooking, of glass beads, and woven cloth. Rum, of course, was in a new category (Zimmerman: 1974). If it is possible to express as a theme this Delaware dependence on manufactured European goods during the first part of the eighteenth century, it might be: "It is essential to receive certain goods from the Europeans, in order to obtain and prepare foods, be properly, attractively, and adequately dressed, and compete with other groups and protect one's group from them."

3. Perhaps equally important to this material concern was a personal matter. This is the importance of individual wishes which seems to be shared throughout much of the northeast woodland culture area (Kroeber, 1947; Hallowell, 1945; 1946; Spindler and Spindler, 1957). Much attention has been paid to the psychological workings of dream-interpretation and wish-fulfillment, especially among the Iroquoian speakers (A.F.C. Wallace, 1951; 1952; 1969). There is good reason to believe that this was shared in a general way by the Lenape (Lilly, 1954; Newcomb, 1956; Spindler and Spindler, 1957). This strongly personal individualism was true for both sexes, but was perhaps more noticeable in the men, because it was so important a part of their self-conception as emotionally restrained warriors. Certainly Delawares in both the seventeenth century (before their subservience to the Iroquis) and the eighteenth century (after they had reasserted their independence) showed that they shared in the general Eastern Woodland complex of controlled interpersonal relations and warrior bravery/torture of captives (Knowles, 1940; Hallowell, 1946). We might express this theme, then, "It is important that each individual's desires be known, understood, and satisfied, that friction between community members be avoided, and it is particularly important for a man to be able to stay true to his personal honor."

4. There is yet another theme which Delaware culture shared with many other cultures which stress the importance of hunting and gathering, and that is generosity, especially among kin. This is particularly noted among many North American Indians, certainly in the Eastern Woodland Culture Area. In so far as it affects our analysis, this value could be stated: "A person or group who is in a position to share resources, goods, or space with others, should do so."

COINCIDENT THEMES JOINTLY SHARED IN LENAPE AND ANGLO-AMERICAN CULTURES

As I mentioned in starting this section, these are in no way exhaustive lists of major emphases in the cultures, but only attempts to characterize briefly those important for our analysis. This next set of themes are those which are sufficiently similar in both Delaware and colonial culture so that we can express them in one statement. I have placed them here, in effect "between" those of the Indian and the White culture, to follow the examples worked out by Malinowski (1945), although I differ in putting the aboriginal culture first, and the encroaching European culture third for this analysis. In effect, the shared themes of this middle ground are Malinowski's *"Common Measure"* or *"Common Factor* of interests and intentions" (1945: chap. VI).

1. The first and certainly most important is the high value placed by members of both societies on maintaining a friendly peaceable relationship. Like most cultural themes, it is not without contradictory or limiting forces (Opler, 1945: p. 201; 1968: p. 225), but it is of sufficient primacy so that most other values are clearly secondary. The most concrete expression of this during the eighteenth century was in the diplomatic phrase "the Great Chain of Friendship," which had symbolically linked the Dutch and then English of the Hudson River trade with the Iroquois (Trelease, 1960; 1962; and Conference of 26 July, 1753, *N.Y. Colonial Documents* 6: pp. 808 ff.). The metaphor was extended to the relationship of other colonies with the Five (later Six) Nations (P.A.W. Wallace, 1945; 1961; Jennings, 1974), and was specifically used by Governor Bernard in his 1758 invitation to the Delaware to "make a chain of peace" (*N.J. Archives* 9: p. 126).

2. A second theme is much more specific, because it relates only to those Lenape left in central New Jersey during the mid-eighteenth century, but for them, and for the Anglo-American colonists around them, it was a value in which the two cultural systems agreed. This was that the central Jersey groups should be protected from frontier pressures, by isolation from "the wilder Indians." With specific reference to French-English competition in Pennsylvania, the Iroquois had a saying of general applicability, "You can't live in the woods and stay neutral." This seems to have been how members of the Crosswicks-Cranbury Delaware bands felt, too. Perhaps both cultures would have agreed on some statement such as "the actions of Lenape now living among English Colonists should not be lumped together with those of other Delaware, (and Shawnee, etc.) living beyond the frontier of Anglo-American settlement, nor should they be subject to a situation in which their actions *might* become like those of frontier Indians."

3. A third theme on which there would probably be close agreement concerned self-sufficiency. Undoubtedly the two cultures would express this theme differently in

that the Lenape who settled at Brotherton probably hoped to be able to have a bit of both worlds—"good hunting" (and gathering), and some farm produce and income in New Jersey provincial currency from the sawing of lumber, while at least some Whites hoped that the Brotherton Indians would eventually become farmers capable of feeding themselves. But both would have agreed that: "It is important for a group of Delaware to be able to support themselves, and not to be dependent on Anglo-American largesse."

4. The fourth pertinent value-emphasis in Lenape and White culture is that an intercessor or protector was needed to prevent various kinds of encroachment by aggressive and competitive Anglo-Americans on the interests of the Delaware. Specifically, this took the form of the Indians asking the government for protection, and of the governors appointing John Brainerd first as missionary, then as "Superintendent and Guardian," at Brotherton. Unfortunately, we have no documentation for Lenape concurrence in this, and can only infer their agreement, but it follows from the dependence they did express on the friendliness and protection of the provincial government, and their apparent acceptance of first David and then John Brainerd. Perhaps both cultures would say, "A group of Lenape living in the midst of growing Anglo-American farms and villages needs, as a special protector, a White man who has some influence with and understanding of law and the authorities."

5. One more highly stressed value which affected the intercultural relationship and on which some significant agreement probably occurred was the importance of keeping an agreement once made. Whites speak of "the sanctity of contract," and Teedyuscung at the Easton Conference of July 28, 1756, said "Whish Shicksy . . . Whish Shiksy [Be strong . . . be strong]" in pleading that the promises made there by the Pennsylvania government should be kept (*Pennsylvania Colonial Records* 8: p. 209). Other Lenape used this forceful expression in a similar sense in treaty conferences with Anglo-Americans during this same period (Thwaites, 1904: 1: pp. 211, 220, 227). Certainly there were gross deviations from the norm of behavior by which this theme is expressed in each culture, but the value was very strong in both cultures, despite any human failures. In theory, it was particularly strong between groups. "A treaty between two sovereign groups is a compelling obligation on members of each group."

THEMES IN ANGLO-AMERICAN CULTURE

1. Parallel to the theme and variants in Delaware culture which derive from emphasis on hunting in a Horticultural/Hunting-and-Gathering economy is the extremely important themal complex related to farming for Anglo-Americans. Succinctly put the central value here is that: "The Good Life is that of a yeoman farmer." From this, as in the Lenape case, a number of things follow. The first of these is that the proper role for a man is farming, which includes stock breeding and raising, but does not usually, in the most general formulation, include large-scale herding, especially to the exclusion of farming.

This White male role is not only that of primary food producer, or of the contributor of the most highly valued food. It is the role of exclusive food producer or "breadwinner," so that his wife is relegated to the role of food preparer, "home-maker," bearer of children, and practicer of various handicrafts. The White man, then, is more dominant in his culture than the Delaware man in his. Farming is, of course, to be conducted industriously, and in a certain spirit of competition. The most respected farmer in an area is the most successful. One should strive to improve one's economic situation, by more intense and wiser farming, and by producing ever greater surpluses of food and more numerous descendants. In this sense the general principle underlying the specific activity of farming was that a man should "husband" his various resources, invest them wisely in the exploitation of the available environment and seek to "be successful," the measure of which was the degree of growth of his operation.

A second result of the primary emphasis on economically successful farming, in an already diversified, technologically advanced, and incipiently urbanized society, is that a farm is a permanent establishment, with a relatively expensive plant. In theory, one could start "from scratch" and acquire all this by "the sweat of one's brow." In fact, even the most bare-bones pioneering required sophisticated tools and equipment, a solid permanent residence, and a rapidly increasing capital investment in livestock, fencing, and eventually in nearby grain milling capacity, routes of transportation, repair and maintenance specialists (e.g., a smithy), and an on-going proliferation of accessory facilities and services, which could be summed up as the "developing and civilizing" of an area.

Also absolutely essential to farming of this pattern is the concept of "real estate," that is, privately owned land, which "belongs" to the man who farms it. By extension, everything is "owned" by some person, or, in certain circumstances, some group of persons. All livestock is owned, every tree on a piece of property is owned, and where "object ownership" is not practical, then persons own rights, as in river water, for example, where owners of adjacent property have certain "riparian rights" to the use of some of the water that flows past. Ideally, all land and all objects under a given governmental jurisdiction must be owned by someone, whether it be the crown (preferably as little as possible), proprietors (who ideally own only in order to sell to farmers), or individual subjects of the crown, each of whom owns his land outright. A corporate group may have some holdings, such as the building and burial yard held by a church congregation, or a village common, but while there is allowance for such bodies, they are not the basic unit in terms of which this cultural ideal operated. Part of the specialist activity in Anglo-American culture at this time was ancillary to the concept of private ownership of the only "real" thing, land, and of all the other things that grew or stood on or derived out of that land. Most of the legal system, all the surveying, and much of the fiscal and governmental activity were tied to this. In the mid-eighteenth century, only commerce, that is, the buying, selling, storing, and conveying of goods, was a real competition to landowning/farming as an economic activity. In time, this specific activity would outstrip farming, but the underlying presumptions were the same.

2. Again placed in juxtaposition to a second major theme among the Delawares is the attitude among Anglo-Americans toward the aboriginal cultures with which they were in contact, and which they tended to lump. Perhaps most New Jersey colonists would not have gone quite as far as Dr. Johnson when he said "one set of Savages is like another" (Hill, 1904: p. 356), but in general they were likely to differentiate Indians mostly along political lines, and not to observe cultural differences. The assumption was that the superiority of the Anglo-American way of life was self-evident, and therefore the continued existence of another culture pattern in their midst was an anomaly, which would or should be eliminated. I do not mean to say that it was universally assumed that the people who practiced that different way of living should be exterminated. Probably only a very small minority would have subscribed to such beliefs. After all, there was almost universal repugnance (among the literate classes, at least) toward the behavior of New Jersey's few Indian murderers, or at the killings perpetrated in the next decade by the Paxton Boys of the Pennsylvania frontier. I am not trying to characterize the attitudes of frontiersmen, but of the largely secure and settled province of New Jersey, although it must be remembered that Tom Quick, the pathological "Indian Slayer," came out of the raids and reaction in the Minisink country of the Upper Delaware in the 1760's and after (Bevier, 1846; Quinlan, 1851; Bross, 1887; Gardiner, 1888; Crumb, 1936). What I believe is a fair characterization is that the significant body of Anglo-American colonial opinion in New Jersey was that the anomaly of Indians persisting in the midst of the province ought to and would be ended by the conversion of these Lenape into "orderly and useful Subjects." The process involved was to be cultural, but it was largely conceived of in religious terms, which is not surprising considering the pervasive influence of religious affiliation at the time.

3. A third major complex of beliefs relates to the special community inhabited by Indians. Here we are dealing not only with a very specific matter, rather than with general principles, but also with one for which there was little or no precedent. It is perhaps less accurate to characterize the following as themes. Rather, they are expressions of themes, but since they all focus on the issue created by Brotherton, they are conveniently grouped here.

The first item is that since all land should be owned, preferably by private individuals, the existence of a communally occupied tract was as much of an anomaly as the persistence of a culture which valued hunting and gathering in the midst of a farming society. Brotherton was therefore doubly ill-fitting. A second item was that as long as Brotherton was there and different, it should receive a different status. This was recognized in making it tax exempt. It is noteworthy, however, that Brotherton had a somewhat different legal basis than later federal reservations, and so its tax-exempt status was different. Most nineteenth-century federal Indian treaties contained clauses in which the native group in question "reserved" for itself a portion of its previous territory, while ceding the remainder to the United States Government in response to certain pressures and in return for which certain goods and services were to be supplied. The land on these reservations was tax exempt because each reservation was the remains of a sovereign state, albeit, in Chief Justice Marshall's phrase, a "domesticated foreign nation . . . in a state of pupilage" (*Cherokee Nation* v. *State of Georgia,* 5 March, 1831, V Peters I).

Brotherton, on the other hand, was purchased with funds raised under a public lottery authorized by the legislature. The land had belonged to the Anglo-Americans for two or three generations, and there was no contested Delaware claim to any part of it. After purchase, it belonged to the governor and his successors, that is, to the province or later state of New Jersey, but was expressly limited to use by and for the benefit of the central New Jersey Lenape. This was agreed to by these Delawares, in lieu of their various unresolved claims. Thus while many federal reservations represented a remnant of politically independent territory, still only partly dependent in a legal sense, Brotherton was a provincial tract of land, the use of which the Lenape accepted in foregoing other claims.

The third item follows directly from provincial recognition of the special, tax-exempt status of the land. This is that the community to be established should not depend on involuntary public support. The tax debt of the province was already high, because of expenses of the war (Larrabee, 1970). Rather, this should be supported by lottery and subscription, because it was a charity. In general, at this time, most of what we now refer to as "welfare costs" were supported by voluntary contribution. A major theme of Anglo-American culture is expressed in this. If one is fortunate in material possessions, one ought to be generous in supporting the needy. It is the charitable and Christian thing to do. But it must be a voluntary offer, to meet the moral obligation. One should not be made to do it, for then it would be merely a tax, and one could not exercise the

God-given opportunity to do the right thing because one consciously chose it. In other words, free will, and the choice to do good or to sin, required in this case that there be a real choice. And it is clear that Brotherton was a charity as far as most New Jersey colonists were concerned.

4. Out of this grows a fourth major theme, that of "obligation." Despite the anomolous position of Brotherton in terms of culture and property rights, numerous citizens of New Jersey felt that there was a sacred trust. The feeling is certainly related to conscience, and shows that many Whites did have a sense that, in some way, the Delawares had been taken advantage of up to that point in time. Obligation, in this sense, is honor, as in Helen Hunt Jackson's *Century of Dishonor* (1881). In her view it was not the Indians who had been morally hurt. They had only suffered betrayal, physical harm, and in many cases death. Rather it was the honor of the White people of the United States culture which had been tarnished. Modifying this sense of obligation was the belief that as long as the Delawares had some property, the costs of liquidating that property should be taken out of the sale price. Apparently the status of Brotherton, owned by the state rather than by the Indians, was not fully recognized.

IV. PROBLEMS INTERFERING WITH EXPRESSION OF THESE THEMES

CONFLICT IN DELAWARE CULTURAL THEMES

The first paradox is that the traditional subsistence pattern, around which a complex of themes were centered, was becoming progressively more difficult to sustain, as larger parts of New Jersey were used by Anglo-American farmers. This produced a situation in which there were hunters who could not readily find territory to hunt. There was also, as the law of 1757 showed, competition from White and Black hunters and trappers. It is a fairly safe guess that the law did more to record the existence of this conflict than it did to resolve it. Incidentally, the same men who were increasingly frustrated in finding good hunting were also prevented from occupying themselves in their other primary traditional occupation, warfare, but that will be discussed below. Moreover, whatever pressures there were for acculturation would have urged these men to become farmers, which to them was a feminine occupation. All of this certainly meant that there were greater personal stresses for the Lenape men in the mid-eighteenth century than for the women.

Of great importance at this time was being on friendly terms with the White culture, and particularly of receiving European goods that were now necessities. However, as fur-bearing game in New Jersey disappeared, the Lenape had less to trade with the colonists, at the very time that they felt greater need for the manufactured objects they could obtain only with this trade.

Before contact the political situation had apparently been one of partial autonomy for village bands, within larger political units and totemic kin-groups. It was under such conditions that the strongly felt needs of each individual were expressed and met. Now this theme of individual independence was threatened, or at least limited, by two developments. The first was that as the main body of Lenape moved west from the lower Hudson and Delaware valleys to the middle Susquehanna, and then to the upper Ohio, in the first half of the eighteenth century, they developed a sense of tribal identity. Various leaders now appeared as power became more consolidated, culminating in the French and Indian War Chiefs Shingas and Captain Jacobs and in Teedyuscung who was able at least to claim to be "King of the Delawares" (Wallace, 1949; Lilly, 1954; Newcomb, 1956; Hunter, 1960; Weslager, 1972). There were intergroup political frictions involved during this process, as well as limitations on the traditional independence of the individual. It seems likely that the Unami Lenape who stayed near Crosswicks and Cranbury and eventually became the Brotherton band intentionally avoided the political pressures of other Delawares. Personal conflicts may have seemed fewer in an isolated cultural enclave in Anglo-American New Jersey than when subject to intensive peer-pressures from other Lenape, as was the case in western Pennsylvania.

Closely related to this is the degree of personal prestige lost by Delawares, especially men, during the period of Iroquois dominance. The Unami seem to have been defeated but not displaced in fur-trade wars by the Susquehannock by about 1640 (Neill, 1876: pp. 30–31; Holm, 1834: p. 158), and the latter in turn were defeated and driven south by the Iroquois by the mid-1670's (Hunt, 1940: pp. 142–144; Hoffman, n.d.: pp. 2, 30–31, 53; 1964: p. 231). The Lenape, or at least the Unami portion, may have fallen heir to the Iroquois after 1674, or a separate arrangement may have been made. At any rate, Iroquois domination was recognized by the Delawares possibly as early as 1680 (Hithquoquean, 1694; Gov. John Evans, 1707; Scollitchy, 1712, in: *Pennsylvania Colonial Record* 1: p. 410; 2, pp. 402–403, 571–574). A crucial aspect of the relationship between the Five Nations and the Delawares was the ascription to the latter of the special role of "Women." It is not easy to translate this because English does not have a term equivalent to the archaic Iroquoian word *Gantowisas,* now an Iroquoian ceremonial term, and probably specifically appropriate only in their matrilineal system where respected elder women were peacemakers and electors of male leaders within a community (P. A. W. Wallace, 1961: p. 57; Fenton, 1971: pp. 138–139).

There has been considerable discussion of the Lenape role as "Women" in their relationship with the Iroquois (Weslager, 1943: pp. 14–23; 1944: pp. 381–388;

A. F. C. Wallace, 1947; 1949: pp. 37, 195–196; Newcomb, 1956: p. 85; Hoffman, n.d.: pp. 34–36; P. A. W. Wallace, 1961: pp. 56–57; Jennings, 1974). At first the Delaware role seems to have been a respectable, if subservient, one in the expanding system of Iroquoian influence, and they were not dispossessed by the Iroquois, but were allowed to stay in their original territory and sell it piecemeal to the White proprietors of New Jersey and Pennsylvania, following which various Delaware groups moved north and west. For a generation following the formation of Pennsylvania the Delaware role was probably strengthened, at least in that province. By the 1730's and 40's, however, Lenape in Pennsylvania were becoming unwilling to move further, and the Penn family enlisted Iroquois assistance during the famous "Walking Purchase" of 1737 and the subsequent 1742 enforcement of its terms (Thayer, 1943: p. 183; P. A. W. Wallace, 1945: pp. 96–99; 1961: pp. 142–143; A. F. C. Wallace, 1949: pp. 19–39; Hunter, 1960: pp. 6, 81; 1961; 1974 a: pp. 72–73). It is at this time that the definition of the Delawares as "Women" came to be an insult and a prohibition of independent action, as illustrated in the scolding given by Canasetego, an Onondaga chief, to assembled Lenape at Pennsbury (just across the Delaware from the Crosswicks area) on July 12, 1742.

You ought to be taken by the Hair of the Head and shak'd severely, till you recover your Senses and become Sober; ... But how come you to take upon you to Sell Land at all? We conquer'd You, we made Women of you, you know you are Women, and can no more sell Land than Women ... (*Pennsylvania Colonial Records* 4: p. 579).

When hostilities erupted on the frontier in 1755, the Delaware had not been involved at first. It was reported to the proprietory government of Pennsylvania that participating with the French in Braddock's defeat were "not one of the Delawares" (Kenny, 1913). However, cut off from English trade and dependent on the French, the western Lenape were making attacks by the end of 1755. By doing so, the main body of Delawares was, in effect, declaring its independence from Iroquois control. Following this the imagery of the role of Women became even more highly colored. Sir William Johnson tried to placate these Delawares in 1756, saying that he had "concluded this treaty by taking off the Petticoat, or that invidious name of Women from the Delaware Nation" (*Pennsylvania Archives,* ser. 2: 6: p. 453). The Iroquois still thought differently, and Chief Newcastle warned the Delawares in the summer of 1756:

You will remember that you are our women, our Forefathers made you so, and put a Petty Coat on you, and charged you to be true to us and lye with no other man. But of late you have suffer'd the String yt ty'd your Pettycoat to be cut loose by the French and you lay with them and so became a common Bawd, in which you did very wrong and deserved Chastisement. ... We advise you not to act as a Man yet but be first instructed by us and do as we bid you (P.A.W. Wallace, 1945: p. 450).

At the same time, Teedyuscung was bitterly accusing the governor of Pennsylvania of acceding to the Iroquois definition of the Lenape, saying, "the Five Nations used to lett him sett out of doors like women; if the Five Nations still make him a woman, they must; but what is the reason the Governor makes him a woman?" (*Pennsylvania Colonial Record* 7: p. 217).

By 1758 the Lenape in western Pennsylvania were proudly proclaiming, *"we are now men,* and not so easily frightened" by the invoking of Iroquois power (Thwaites, 1904: 1: pp. 201–203). Whatever the original sense of the special relationship, the role had become a source of insults by the 1740's and an intolerable burden to Delaware men by the 1750's. Certainly it would produce a substantial internal conflict in any man who thought and felt in terms of the stoic, restrained, amiable, yet insistently personally independent mode of a hunter and warrior of the eastern woodlands.

CONFLICT IN AREA OF SHARED VALUES

Even in those themes where Lenape and Anglo-American attitudes seemed to coincide, there were certain practical considerations which interfered with satisfying the interests of both sides. In the first two areas of common ground there was probably a reasonable degree of success. The relationship between the Brotherton band and its White neighbors was kept peaceful, despite raids on the Minisink frontier during Pontiac's War and again during the American Revolution. This very fact shows that isolation from "the wilder Indians," probably desired by the Brotherton Unami as much as by the Anglo-Americans of New Jersey, was effective.

It is in the third area that agreement was not sufficient for success. Good will and a shared desire for Brotherton to become a self-sustaining community economically were not enough. Even to the limited degree that the Delawares were adopting European farming methods and shifting their subsistence base, a constant source of manufactured goods and money was needed, and the 1762 plea to the legislature for money to repay the debt for "nails" was never answered. In short, there was no follow-up financial support of the community, once Brotherton had been established. The Whites were no longer under the immediate pressure of Indian War, and the felt obligation had been adequately met with the creation of the reserved area. As a result, with no cash income, the Lenape could not have practiced an Anglo-American farming pattern even if they had had the requisite values and skills. This was what ultimately led to the leasing of the land, the need for fiscal management by Commissioners, and finally to the sale of the assets. It is a pattern repeated many times in North America, with lack of capital one factor preventing the reservation Indians from utilizing their resources in a way acceptable to Anglo-Americans, so that the only "solution" is for the Anglo-Americans to "manage" and "develop" them, often ostensibly for the Indians' benefit (Jorgenson, 1972; White, 1974).

Another factor where shared ideals did not produce desired results was in the role of the protector. There is no specific statement to this effect, but actions speak clearly. John Brainerd seems to have lost interest in his mission, and to have turned increasing attention to Anglo-American churchgoers, because there was little to show for his work. His hopes for rapidly producing a congregation of sober, industrious Presbyterian farmers were disappointed, and although he never completely forsook the Brotherton community, his heart does not seem to have been in it after about the mid-1760's. Here there was failure, rather than conflict, in a shared theme.

Finally, there was the problem of keeping agreements. This is valued in both cultures, but a person expressing an intent to follow through does not always have the capability. Governor Bernard was undoubtedly sincere in his promises of continued support for Brotherton, but he was succeeded by other governors, and colonial governors could not necessarily predict or control the actions of the legislature, nor of the royal government in London. In this sense, the shared value on keeping agreements may have been almost a liability because when members of both cultures saw that the agreements were not being kept, the values were violated for both sides.

There is one final area in which the coinciding of themes was disfunctional to the success of the Brotherton community, but in this case it was a shared theme which worked all too well. I have included it here because its demoralizing effect is important in analyzing the failure of Brotherton, although technically it is simply a sixth area of agreement between the cultures. This is the perception by members of both Delaware and Anglo-American cultures that the Indians were dwindling in number, vitality, and importance, and that both the culture and the individuals were doomed to extinction. We might call it the "vanishing Indian" theme, and it is very important in explaining motives. To the Delawares, whose relatives were moving farther away, it meant that all the larger extensions of their social system were disappearing. To the Anglo-Americans, whether they were sympathetic to the problems of the Brotherton band, or resented its presence, it meant that the anomaly presented by the people of this ethnic enclave hunting, fishing, and gathering for a living, and holding land in common, was a self-canceling problem. Some Whites tried to alleviate suffering, save souls, or save individuals by turning them into "sober subjects." Others may have been impatient at the length of time it was taking for the cultural abnormality to disappear, but as long as the Anglo-Americans agreed with Bartholemew Calvin's characterization of the remnants of the Brotherton band as "old and weak and poor" and "a wasted, yet grateful people"

this assumption would affect all their actions (Barber and Howe, 1844: p. 511).

CONFLICT IN ANGLO-AMERICAN CULTURAL THEMES

There are a number of conflicts within the Anglo-American cultural themes, partly due to the very complexity of the society, and also several impediments to the full expression of other themes, due to the situation of the New Jersey colonists and citizens in the latter half of the eighteenth century. One of these is that the care of the Brotherton community was entrusted to the missionary John Brainerd by both provincial officials and by concerned supporters in New Jersey, Pennsylvania, New York, and in the British Isles, but that such concern was not necessarily felt by the immediately surrounding Anglo-American farming community. These local settlers seem to have resented the creation of Brotherton, or at least its persistence after an initial surge of feeling that the reservation was a solution to the mid-eighteenth-century "Indian Problem," just as farmers had earlier complained of the presence of Indians at Bethel. The conflict, then, is between a superintendent-missionary, appointed and supported by distant sources of power and social conscience, and a local community of farmer-property owners, who feel immediately threatened by the anomalous presence of the Indian group and the reservation. In the case of Brotherton, this conflict seems to have been at least partially muted by Brainerd's active work in ministering to the surounding Whites as actively as to Brotherton Lenape.

A problem clearly related to the complexity of Anglo-American culture, in this and in many parallel cases, is interdenominational dispute. Here it has been suggested that there was friction between the Quakers and the Presbyterians. The former had a long-term interest in establishing good relations with the Lenape, treating them with Brotherhood, and avoiding open conflict. Moreover, the Friends were very influential among the large property holders, especially in West Jersey, and had an important voice in the Assembly. The latter were fairly new on the scene in New Jersey, but were riding the emotional religious wave of the Great Awakening, and very actively preaching to Indians and Anglo-Americans alike, especially through such dedicated missionaries as the Brainerd brothers. The Presbyterians had important support from the British government and, with the creation of the College at Princeton, were also influential in New Jersey.

Conflicts which are of apparently only minor importance regarding Brotherton are those between the proprietors of the land in East and West Jersey and the royal government represented by the crown-appointed governor, and the broader manifestation of this problem in the growing difficulties between the Anglo-American colonists in general and the mother country. While both of these became major focuses of political

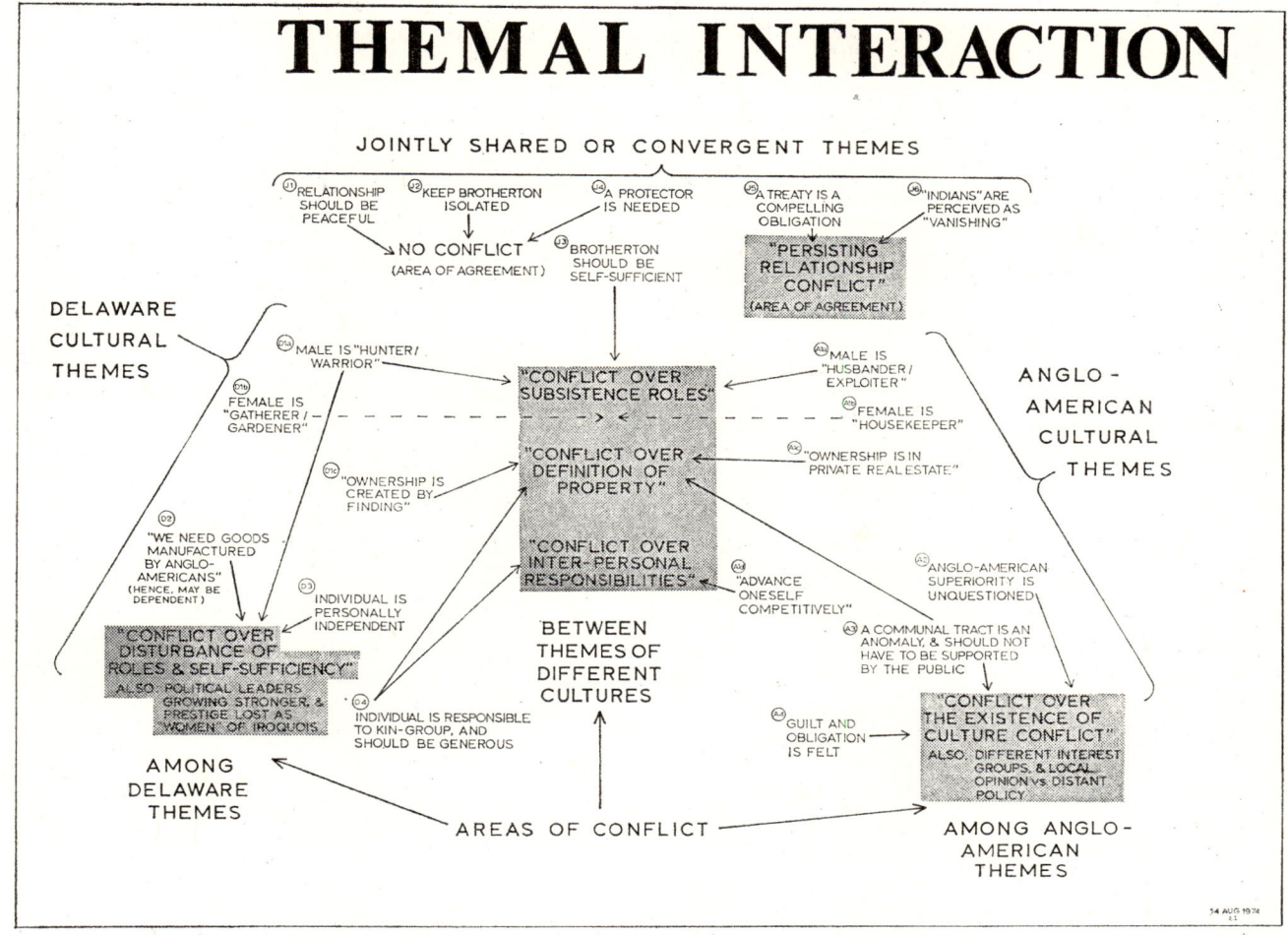

Fig. 1.

attention, leading eventually to the War of Independence, the ensuing constitutional crises, and the creation of the system of state and federal government, they do not seem to have materially affected the relationship between the Anglo-Americans and the Brotherton Lenape. Possibly the retention of a position of strong royal governor throughout the entire eighteenth century would have meant more consistent support for Brotherton, but that is mere supposition. The 1760's saw the British imperial government both taking real steps toward considering Indian groups as crown subjects and protecting their interests against the pressures of other subjects, and at the same time callously disregarding the needs of Indians in matters of trade, support gifts, and military policy (Gipson, 1958–1969; Jacobs, 1950; Shy, 1965; McNickle, 1973). It is doubtful that Brotherton would have fared much differently under some other governmental arrangement, as long as the dominant culture surrounding it shared the Anglo-American value system.

DISCUSSION OF DIAGRAM "THEMAL INTERACTION" (fig. 1)

The diagram represents the relationship between various themes in graphic form. There are six major foci of conflict. Three of these come from differences in values relating to similar subject matter, and occur in a central location which is designated "area of conflict between themes of different cultures." The first of these three foci is "conflict over subsistence roles," which is occasioned by the belief shared by both groups that the Brotherton community should be self-supporting, but with radically different perceptions of the male role in providing that subsistence. The Delaware viewed a man's position as one of a "hunter and warrior." The Anglo-American assumption was that a male should provide support by laboring, accumulating capital, and controlling natural forces to his advantage, most typically in the eighteenth century as a farmer.

A second conflict focus arising because of points of view differing between the two cultures is the "conflict over definition of property." This very important source of trouble is the result of the extreme difference between the Delaware belief that a person makes a thing his own by finding it and using it, and the very strong Anglo-American emphasis on legally documented ownership of measured parcels of land, and of all living things on each such piece of "real estate," by private individuals. Other values contributing to this focus of conflict were the requirement in Delaware culture that a person should be generous and share his findings with others, especially within the kinship-based group to which he is responsible, and the anomalous position in the Anglo-American legal and economic private property system of a tract held in common by a group. The third focal point for conflict between cultural views occurs over "interpersonal responsibilities." Here the Delaware's allegiance to his kin group is opposed to the Anglo-American's drive to advance himself in competition with his peers.

These three foci of conflict are not surprising, because we expect differences in the value systems of two cultures to be readily apparent in some cases, but it is instructive in this diagram to see exactly where these conflicts do occur, and to show that sometimes more than just two opposing themes are involved, as in the first case, "subsistence roles," where agreement by both groups that the Brotherton reservation community should be economically self-supporting actually exacerbates the contrast between Delaware and Anglo-American role-models for adult males. It is also interesting to note that some potential conflicts, such as between adult female roles, never become significant.

Interestingly, additional points of conflict which seriously affect the relationship between the two societies can occur entirely within the themal systems of each culture, and even among the themes which both share as part of their intercultural relationship. For example, the changes brought about by the increasing Delaware dependence on trade goods, and the awareness of this, challenges both the strong theme of personal independence of will and the male role as self-sufficient provider/protector. This is labeled "conflict over disturbance of roles and self-sufficiency." Adding to this is the insult felt by Delaware males during the period when the Iroquois controlled their foreign affairs and made "women" of them, and also the stress which developed in a lineage-organized social system as political consolidation occurred under pressure from Anglo-American and Iroquois domination. Strong leaders rose who had widespread following among the members of a society which was just becoming conscious of itself as the "Delaware Tribe." Unquestionably this was disturbing to Lenape who still felt strong personal independence, and primary loyalty to their kin-group. In this way the very existence of the relation between the two cultures, and the complicating presence of the Iroquois in the fur-trade imperial-diplomacy of eighteenth-century North America, cause a focus of conflict within Delaware culture.

A focus also appeared among Anglo-American themes, where the sense of superiority was not only taken for granted, but seemed additionally confirmed by the melting away which is expressed as the sixth convergent theme, that "Indians" are perceived as "Vanishing." However, another Anglo-American cultural theme is found pervasively throughout Western Christian Civilization. This is a general feeling of "guilt and obligation," which in this relationship takes the specific form of assuming responsibility both for the decline of the Delawares and for the maintenance of the small remnant at Brotherton. The obligation to "keep" the Brotherton community, partly in penance for having been the cause of their present low state, is in direct contradiction to the feeling that communal occupation of a tract of land is simply wrong, because all property should be privately held, and that it is doubly wrong to support such an anomaly publicly. It is also at odds with the belief that the superiority of Anglo-American culture is so self-evident that members of the lower-order Delaware way of life should welcome the opportunity to become Anglo-American farmers. I have labeled this as a focus of conflict which exists because of the very fact of "the existence of culture conflict." In other words, the mere presence of the "other" culture in contact with the New Jersey colonists brought forth contradictory feelings of disapproval and guilt, of desire to see the Indians cease their different way of life and accept the values of Anglo American culture and yet also of a desire to comfort and support them.

A final, and perhaps most paradoxical, focus of conflict occurs in the area where themes are convergently held by both cultures. We might expect that where both sides agree on something, at least here there will be no trouble. However, both cultures believed strongly in sanctity of contract, particularly where this involved diplomatic relations between sovereign groups expressed in treaties, and both cultures were, during this period, also acutely conscious of "The Vanishing Indian." The perpetuity stated in the treaty relationship was belied by the belief that soon there would be no more Delawares, and so the permanent relationship agreed upon by both was hollow. In fact, the Brotherton Delawares were, for a long time during the eighteenth and early nineteenth centuries, in the process of disappearing as a recognizably separate cultural enclave, and yet had not finished disappearing as late as the final payment by the New Jersey legislature in 1832. Thus the "persisting relationship" itself, always expressed as if it would last forever, yet always perceived to be in the process of canceling itself out, and continuing in this contradictory state, was a source of conflict even where Lenape and Anglo-Americans agreed upon the terms of reference.

The six foci identified here create the dynamic points where themes interact. It is the interplay of values around these foci that helps to cause the sequence of

V. PARALLELS AND SEQUENCE

IDENTIFICATION OF PARALLELS

Any person reading this who is familiar with the general relationship between the European powers and colonies and their successor, the federal government of the United States, and the aboriginal peoples within its borders, or with any particular relationship between one Indian group and Anglo-Americans, will already have seen many similarities with this particular eighteenth-century effort. What is proposed for this section is to list these parallel aspects, and then to attempt to draw a generalized sequence chart. In the final portion of this paper I shall try to explain why these parallels exist, and why the sequence is as it is.

1) *Land sales bring dissatisfaction, even when the Indians feel that they have been paid what they expected.*

This is a commonplace in North America that scarcely needs further comment here, except to mention that there is a voluminous literature (Brown, 1970; Collier, 1947; Debo, 1940; Hallet, 1959; Jackson, 1881; LaFarge, 1940; McLeod, 1928; McNickle, 1957, 1973; Merriam, 1928). There are similarities in Canada and in other parts of the world also (Elkin, 1951; Firth, 1929; Malinowski, 1945; McNickle, 1973; Service, 1954, 1955).

2) *Indians and Whites are uneasy neighbors.*

After a sale Indians often stayed in the area, frequently on the piece of land sold to the Whites, and continued living as before, until the natural resources were no longer easily available because of European economic development. Many differences in worldview are important in this item, but free use of found resources, ownership of standing growth and roving livestock, free access, and trespass across property lines, are among the major points of conflict. For example, it was the killing of Thomas Matthews's hogs by refugee Susquehannocks which was the occasion for Bacon's Rebellion in Virginia in 1676 (Washburn, 1957). Maintenance of fencing was also an issue in seventeenth-century New England (Vaughn, 1965). At the end of the nineteenth century this was still true in California, when White ranchers killed a band of Yahi Indians who had been raiding their stock (T. Kroeber, 1967).

The Brotherton story provides a clear expression from both cultures of this conflict between territory hunters and livestock-owning, fenced-field agriculturalists.

3) *Dissatisfaction pressures build on both sides with no institutionalized means of relief.*

Even in cases where attempts were made to establish a regular relationship with frequent meetings, as in colonial New York or Pennsylvania, there seems to have been no way to alleviate the conflict which grew between the members of the two cultures, except through major and abrupt rearrangements of power. The only peaceful relationships maintained for any length of time appear to have depended on the Indians melting away, through migration, disease, or other means, from the area where European settlers were increasing in number.

4) *Interests of different Europeans who consciously go out to Indian Communities are often contradictory. Frequently this is apparent in the form of a struggle between traders and missionaries.*

Again, examples are very common. One would be in the Pacific Northwest where the interests of the Hudson's Bay Company clashed with those of both American and English missionaries (Kardas, 1971). The issue is, of course, that many missionary efforts attempt wholesale planned change of the culture of Indians, especially the living pattern, while most traders depend on the maintenance of a hunting economy, although with a transfer of effort from meat animals to fur and hide animals. Early efforts by the Brainerds at Bethel met this kind of white opposition.

5) *A crisis in the relationship precipitates action.*

The corollary seems to be that without a crisis, both sides try to ignore the growing difficulties. It is doubtful whether New Jersey would have sent delegates to any conferences, passed any laws, or established Brotherton, if the French and Indian War had not occurred. A parallel might be the way in which the lengthy, expensive, and inconclusive Seminole War helped produce a major change in the whole direction of federal policy (Manypenny, 1880; Scmeckebier, 1927; Sturtevant in: Leacock and Lurie, 1971).

6) *An adjustment of claims is asked by the Indians.*

A frequent form of the attempt to resolve the situation which the crisis has brought into the open is a "hearing" by the Europeans of the various causes of dissatisfaction among the natives. Land claims rank high on the list. In the formation of Brotherton, they were primary, although this was partly because complaints about trapping competition had been covered by the law of 1757. An example of a similar situation are the councils which preceded the Dakota fighting of the late 1860's and the 1868 peace treaty at Fort Laramie (Mekeel, 1943: pp. 184–187).

7) The Anglo-American government is under pressure from various religious groups to act in a Christian manner.

The Lake Mohonk conferences of the nineteenth century which led to the official establishment of the Board of Indian Commissioners is an example of this. In colonial New Jersey pressure was exerted by both the Friends and the Presbyterians.

8) A treaty is made.

I know of no case north of Spanish territory where this major definition of status occurred at first contact. It is preceded by at least some, and possibly a lengthy, history of trade and often of land sales. Time after time, this treaty-making was the pivotal act defining the relationship between the federal government and the native group. Many bands or tribes went through a number of treaties, as the United States wanted more land, or the removal of that band or tribe to other locations where there would be less conflict with White interests (Foreman, 1932; 1946; Jorgenson in: Waddell and Watson, 1971: pp. 93-95). In other cases there was one treaty, reinterpretations of which have occurred as the power relationships have changed (Larrabee, n.d., a; Debo, 1940; Harper, 1947; McNickle, 1973). Almost by definition treaties between United States and Canadian governments and Indians have presented logical and legal problems, because they were usually made as between two independent sovereign political entities, but the making of them reduced the native polity to the status of a "subject nation" (Kappler, 1904; Merriam, 1928). This is one of the reasons the United States Senate in 1871 refused to ratify any more Indian treaties. The existence of the treaty regularly has become a major factor in building and maintaining group identity, partly because it is the remnant of lost sovereignty. In the case of Brotherton, the agreements of February, August, and September, 1758, ratified and witnessed at the Easton Conference in October, must all be taken together as constituting "the agreement," which is then referred to as late as 1832.

9) Certain rights are reserved.

The hunting and fishing rights in the case of the Brotherton band are a good example of this. Here they were general throughout the province, unlike the more specific fishing at "usual and accustomed places" reserved throughout the Columbia Plateau treaties of 1855 (Larrabee, n.d., a; U.S. Senate Document No. 452, 57th Congress, 1st Session, Article 3). Frequently these became an issue only much later, when intensive Anglo-American resource exploitation occurred.

10) Not all of the treaty or agreement is fulfilled.

Sometimes this is a question of the way in which items or clauses are understood differently by the two parties. It is often a case of the White government failing to provide, for various reasons, all the things to which it has agreed. This was such a commonplace that the "Trail of Broken Treaties" has become a recent rallying cry of Native American movements (Costo, 1970; Hickey, 1973; Josephy, 1973). One specific example which almost exactly duplicates the 1762 Brotherton plea for replacement of their burnt sawmill occurred a century and a quarter later when the Yakima complained that it had been eighteen months since the sawmill promised in their 1855 treaty had burned down, and asked the Bureau of Indian Affairs to replace it (Dickson, 1886: p. 465).

11) A reservation is established.

This is probably the most important single outcome of the majority of United States treaties, and of some Canadian treaties (except in British Columbia—Harper, 1947; Shankel, 1945; McNickle, 1973). As was pointed out earlier, the Brotherton tract was intended as a safe place in which an isolated remnant group of Delawares could live while they were learning to farm like Anglo-Americans, and in this sense it is like other later reservations. The legal status, however, is somewhat different, in that the land had been out of Indian ownership for two generations, it was purchased through a lottery (i.e., by voluntary charitable contribution), and possession was specifically vested in the provincial government. The Lenape received the use of this publicly owned property in return for cession of their other claims in New Jersey, but this legal difference is not really significant in the face of the overwhelming similarities with later reserves.

12) A missionary is named as superintendent.

This was certainly not always the case, but was common, and predominated during periods such as the "Peace Policy" of President Grant's administration (Ekland, 1969; Kelsey, 1917; Schmeckebier, 1927; Wood, 1969). In other cases a missionary was expected to work with an agent or superintendent. A good brief discussion of the role of missionaries in native North American communities has been written by Berkhofer (1963) and specifically for the Delaware by A. F. C. Wallace (1956).

13) Indian requests for additional help are not met.

Not all such requests failed, but frequently there was enough lack of follow-through to discourage the Reservation community. The primary reason for the reduction in Anglo-American interest is that the "Indian Problem" which was urgent during the crisis that preceded the treaty-making was later considered to have been solved. A frequent feeling is that the Indians have just been "given" not only what appears on paper to be ample supplies, but also a large amount of good land. Expenses to the White government have been high, both to meet the crisis (often a war) and for the cost of conferences and the settlement of the crisis by treaty or agreement, so there is resistence to additional outlay. An example which closely parallels this part of the Brotherton experience is the creation, after much hesitation, of what is now the Colville Reservation, and the subsequent placing there of the "hostile" Nez Percé (Ruby and Brown, 1965).

14) *Anglo-Americans want the Indians to live as agriculturalists and conceive of this exclusively in terms of free-holding of individually owned plots of land by male farmer heads-of-family.*

Governor Bernard ordered that new, individual fields be cleared and fenced, and that the land already in cultivation be worked collectively by the Lenape only until "they have acquired themselves separate property, by their own industry" (*N.J. Archives* 9: p. 175). The likeness between this and the latter nineteenth-century reform movement which led to the Dawes Act of 1887 providing universal "allotment in severalty" is striking (Collier, 1947: p. 134; Haas, 1957: pp. 12-16; Hagan, 1956; McNickle, 1957: pp. 10-11; Peterson, 1957: pp. 118-119; Taylor, 1927). Writing during the period of agitation among "concerned easterners" which led to the final passage of that Indian Allotment Act, the New Jersey historian Samuel Allinson made the parallel explicit, when he said of Brotherton, "Persistent industry was not general and they did not become a thriving agricultural people. The tribal fee of land quenches individual enterprise" (1875: p. 46).

15) *Reservation land is leased to White farmers.*

This usually follows a number of seasons in which White officials become discouraged at the failure of the creation of individual property holdings to turn Indians into White farmers, or "undeveloped" land into fenced and cultivated fields. It may, as apparently at Brotherton, be initiated at the suggestion of the reservation Indians themselves, as a means of producing essential cash income for subsistence from the only asset they have. It is interesting that the New Jersey legislature rejected the first request in 1771, and only agreed in 1795. The process was usually proposed as a temporary solution but regularly led, as the New Jersey assembly feared in 1771, to the effective alienation of Indian ownership. It is probable that a number of the 1802 buyers of the parceled land of the Brotherton tract were Anglo-Americans who were already farming Brotherton land under lease, but it would require a detailed scrutiny of many scattered documents to confirm the suspicion that a significant number of lessees became buyers.

16) *Commissioners are appointed by the government to investigate a deteriorating situation on the reservation.*

The classic case of this, on a nationwide scale, is the Board of Indian Commissioners first appointed in 1869 by President Grant's Executive Order (U.S. Board of Indian Commissioners, n.d.).

17) *The Reservation is dissolved using some of the money from the sale of this land to Whites to pay the costs of liquidation.*

The legal reasoning of the Anglo-Americans here seems to have likened the closing of a reservation to settling the estate of a deceased person, or perhaps to a bankruptcy proceeding. As long as there were any assets remaining in some moribund collection of property which was being broken up, those assets should bear the expenses of the process of disintegration of the collection. The similarity is not surprising, since government officials clearly did think of the Indian groups in exactly that sense. The tribes were considered to be both dead, and politically and economically bankrupt. Only some of the individual people remained, so the land once needed for the tribe was now available for distribution to the individual "heirs," with sale of the remainder paying the "costs of probate" and settlement of outstanding debts. Thus the General Allotment Act of 1887 specified that the costs of surveying and distributing the individual parcels of land to the Indians of a reservation, and of the sale of the "surplus" remainder, should come out of the proceeds of that sale. Any profit beyond that was put into general funds, nominally for the Indians, but subject to congressional appropriation.

A process duplicating the liquidation of the Brotherton reserve in 1802 was involved also in the "Termination" policy of the Bureau of Indian Affairs after World War II, which worked most graphically on the factionally divided Klamath and Menomini, again with questions raised about the acquiescence of a majority of Indians (Fenton, 1955; LaFarge, 1957; Watkins, 1957; Lurie in: Leacock and Lurie, 1971: p. 439).

18) *A trust fund remaining after liquidation of the reserve was later paid out.*

For the Klamath and Menomini, this happened after termination of their reservation in 1954 (Stern, 1961). The Brotherton trust fund was held for two decades by the New Jersey State government, and then paid out on petition of the Delawares because the legislature agreed that purchase of a new tract in Wisconsin (ironically, from the Menomini) was a proper use. In all such instances, the Anglo-Americans have felt that this "final payment" would end all government obligation to the descendants of the Indian group with which an agreement had been made.

19) *After distribution of the trust fund which held any profits from the sale of reservation land, the claims of the Indians to any residual rights under the original treaty or agreement are assigned a monetary value and paid off.*

Again, the limitations of the Anglo-American legal and economic system seem to be a critical factor. It is not easy to tolerate the continued existence of rights which are at odds with the general set of cultural assumptions. Therefore, they must be assigned some arbitrary monetary value, and if the natives agree to that valuation, and to transfer of their rights for that amount, the rights can be extinguished for a payment in White man's money. New Jersey patted itself on the back for its generosity in 1832, and implied that the settlement was really a gift, in order not to admit that there necessarily were such residual rights. The moral and legal process which thus ended the continuing but low-level obligation that New Jersey Anglo-Americans felt for the Brotherton Delawares is similar to the rationale used in establishing the Court of Indian Claims (Lurie, 1957). Here, too, there was a need felt by Whites to meet old, vague obligations. This would be done by investigating outstanding claims, assigning to them a "fair market value," and then buying the claims, thus finally giving the various Indian claimants money which the White Americans should have given them long ago. Another mid-twentieth-century example of the same process is the indemnification in cash of Indians for fishing, hunting, and horticultural rights which have been lost owing to large reservoir projects constructed for our own "Hydraulic Society" (Wittfogel, 1959) by the Corps of Engineers, the Bureau of Reclamation, and various regional, local, and private organizations (Relander, 1956; Larrabee, n.d., a; Wilson, 1960). It should be pointed out that in some such cases the compensation was actually paid for the loss of the use of certain locations, or "usual and accustomed sites," rather than for permanent acquisition of the rights to use those places by the public body paying the Indians. In such cases the Indian has retained the rather theoretical privilege of using a particular place again, should the Anglo-American remove the obstruction he has placed there, that is, a dam or the water it impounds. The difference here is between outright purchase of a right to use, and a single payment for the probably permanent rental of the use of a place or area. It is an academic difference as far as the relation between the two cultures is concerned.

The foregoing identification has shown parallels between the creation, maintenance, and liquidation of a special community for remnant Lenape at Brotherton and other events in over three centuries of the Indian-White relationship in North America. The remarkable thing about these similarities is how few of the major events in United States "Indian Relations" cannot be explicitly likened to something in the Brotherton sequence. Possibly two larger events not foreshadowed are "Removal" of the 1820's through the 1840's, and urban "Relocation" of the 1950's. In late 1758 and early 1759 the Delawares were supposed to gather from scattered locations in central New Jersey and concentrate at Brotherton (which not all did), but this was only a pale shadow of the massive and crushing removals of large groups of Indians by United States authorities throughout the nineteenth century. There is no obvious exact parallel to the mid-twentieth-century programs to relocate reservation Indians in large cities, so they could become like modern American factory workers. Of course, the eighteenth- and nineteenth-century model for emulation was a White male farmer, so urbanization and industrialization would hardly have been attempted. In a general sense the similarity is present, in that Whites were trying to remodel Indians to fit White preconceptions of good citizens, or "orderly and useful subjects," in all such cases. (Governor Bernard, 15 June, 1758, *N.J. Archives* 9: p. 175).

GENERALIZED SEQUENCE OF CULTURAL INTERACTION

The identification of parallels has shown that equivalents for all the major events related to Brotherton can be found in other, larger, and subsequent relationships between Indians and Anglo-Americans. A number of authors have divided this overall relationship into what are essentially historical "phases" or "Stages" (Lang, 1961–1962 in: Walker 1972; Leacock in: Leacock and Lurie 1971; Lurie in: Leacock and Lurie, 1971; McNickle, 1973; Oswalt, 1973). In most cases, these are categories into which various cultural behaviors may be characterized. They are not necessarily explanations of that behavior. In contrast, there has been implicit in the foregoing description of the New Jersey relationship the assumption that there is some causal relationship between the New Jersey events, so that the sequence itself is to some degree an explanatory device. It follows that the individual factors so strikingly duplicated in situations simlar to that in late colonial New Jersey may also be assumed to have occurred in a causal relationship to each other, and that the sequence at Brotherton is but one, relatively early, expression of a larger phenomenon—namely, a "generalized sequence of Indian-White relations," as distinguished from a set of historical phases into which the larger relationship may be divided.

Somewhat similar interactive sequences have previously been proposed for culture-contact situations elsewhere in the world during the nineteenth and twentieth centuries (e.g., Firth, 1929; Elkin, 1951), and for specific native cultures or areas in North America (e.g., Mekeel, 1943; Spicer, 1962). Some scholars examining comparative cases of acculturation have specifically rejected the applicability of a single chart such as Elkin's Australian sequence for North America. For example, in summarizing a symposium analysis of culture contact between European or Euro-American and the Yaqui, Rio Grande Pueblos, Mandan, Navajo, Wishram, and Kwakiutl, Spicer has said "nowhere is there evidence that Elkin's sequence is inherent in the contact of European and native cultures and must develop regardless of conditions once contact has been established" (Spicer, 1961: p. 541).

SCHEMATIC VIEW OF
GENERALIZED SEQUENCE
OF CULTURAL INTERACTION
NORTH OF THE RIO GRANDE
EURO-AMERICANS
INDIANS
I NON-DIRECTED CULTURE CONTACT
"EXPLORATION & TRADE"
"CULTURAL AUGMENTATION"
"COLONIZE"
"TRADING COEXISTENCE"
"SERIOUSLY AFFECTED"
"ONLY SLIGHTLY AFFECTED"
"INCORPORATION"
"PEACEFUL DISPLACEMENT"
II OVERT CULTURE CONFLICT
"MILITANT SUBJUGATION"
"RESISTANCE"
"MIGRATION"
TRANSFER OF SOVEREIGNTY FROM INDIANS TO EURO-AMERICANS BY "TREATY"
OR
III DIRECTED CULTURE CONTACT
"MAXIMUM PRESSURE"
"MINIMUM PRESSURE"
"ACCULTURATE AS INDIVIDUALS"
"ACCULTURATE AS A GROUP"
"ACTIVE RECEPTION"
"PASSIVE RECEPTION"
"FUSION"
"TEND TO REACT AS INDIVIDUALS"
"TEND TO REACT AS A GROUP"
(BOTH ABANDONED)
"DISINTEGRATION-REINTEGRATION"
"PERISH"
"REVITALIZE"
"ISOLATION"
UNIFORM TREATMENT TENDS TO PRODUCE AMALGAMATED "INDIAN AWARENESS"
"ASSIMILATE"
"HARD LINE" (ETHNOCENTRISM)
"SOFT LINE" (SOCIAL CONSCIENCE)
"NATIVIZE" (PAN-INDIAN MOVEMENT)
30 AUG. 1974

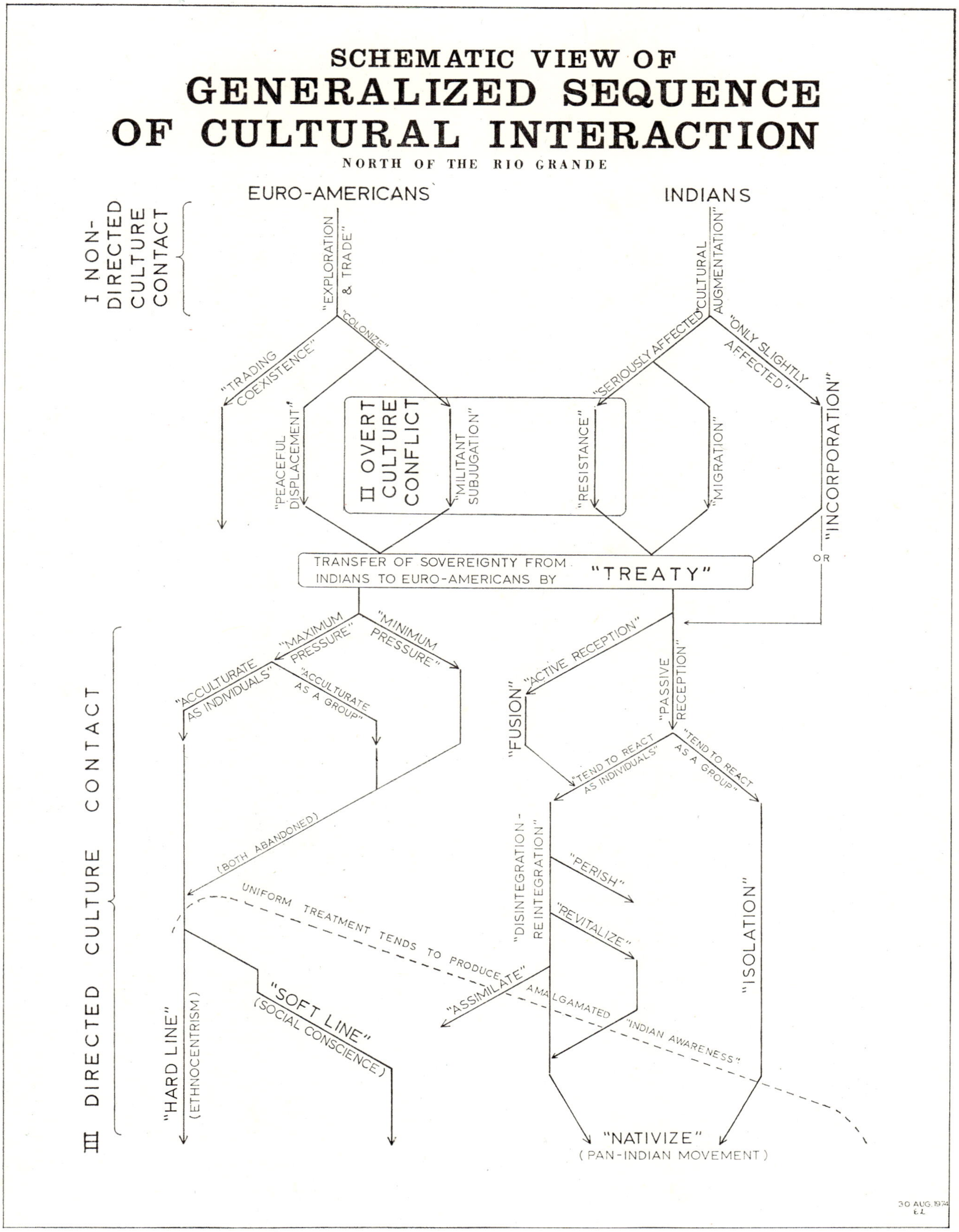

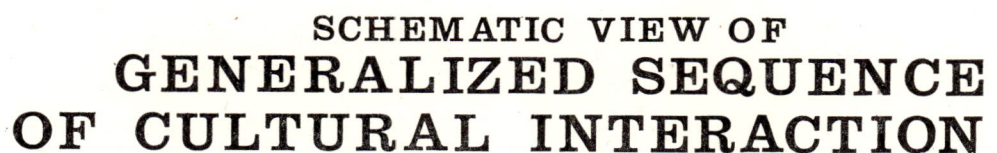

FIG. 2.

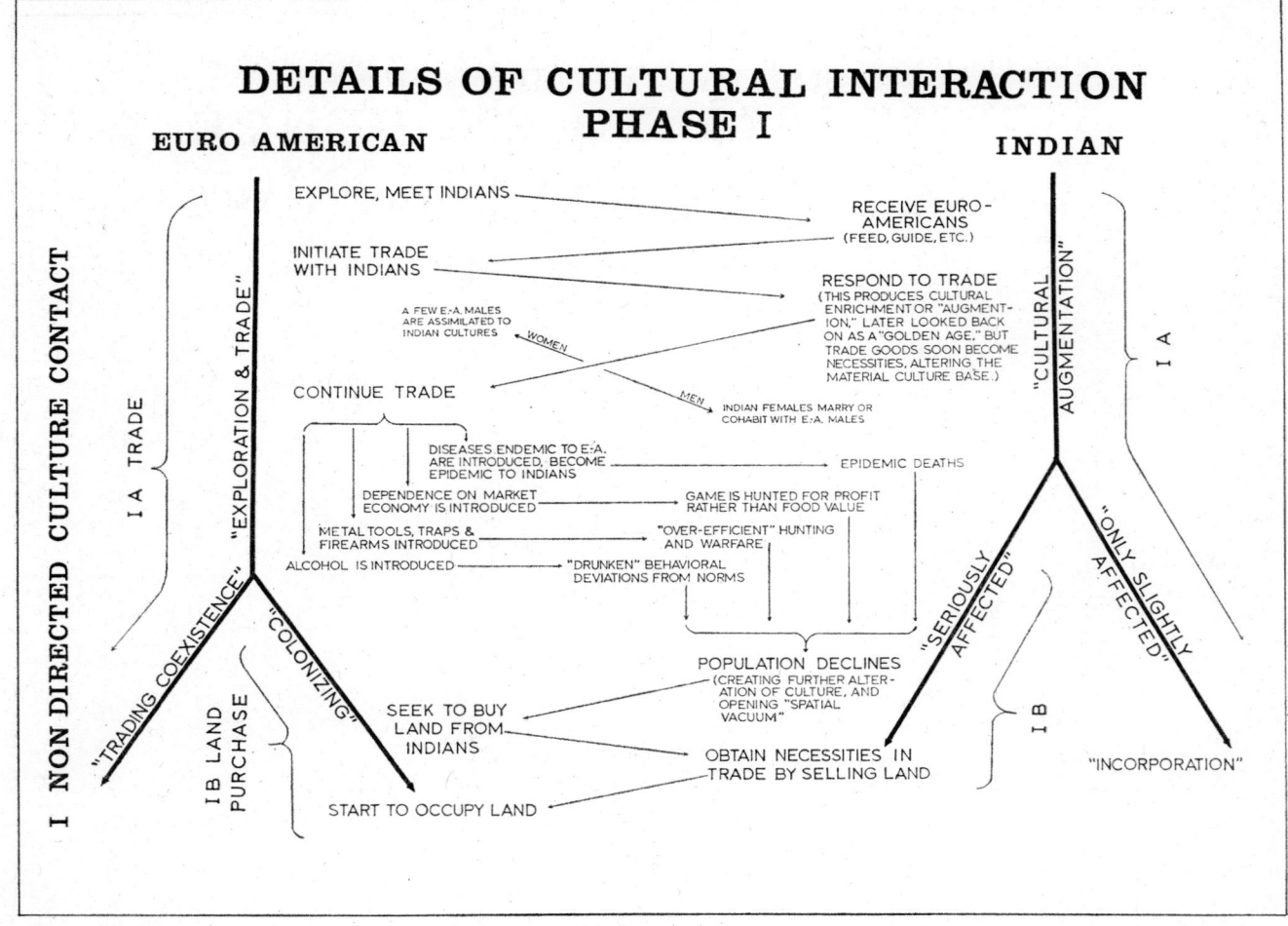

Fig. 3.

Despite the fact that one sequence was not felt appropriate for that sample, we might here attempt to draw up a generalized sequence as an heuristic device with the explicit understanding that this does not pretend to either specific predictive value or to serve as a guide for correcting policy mistakes. Since we are here considering many different cases of culture contact in North America, I have expanded from the term Anglo-American, which was applicable in eighteenth-century New Jersey, to the more general Euro-American. The sequence is first presented in schematic or simplified overall form, and then shown with interactive detail in four charts. For the sake of clarity while showing many specific aspects of interaction, each of these detailed charts is characterized by a phase or subphase of the whole sequence. It should be noted that this is a sequence, not a timetable. There is no implication of any set lengths of time intended for any particular phase or subphase, nor of inevitability in the following of one particular pathway by one culture. The pathways are not linear explanations, but only a way of graphically representing various cultural choices in an interacting system.

COMMENTS ON SEQUENCE

I have followed the terminology of Linton (1940) and Spicer et al. (1961) in referring to culture contact as "nondirected" if one society does not have compulsive power over another (or, having it, fails to use it), and "directed" if one society is in a superordinate position with both desire and ability consciously to induce change in the culture of a subordinate society. This sequence is also like those of Firth (1929) and Mekeel (1943) in finding three major stages, the middle one being a struggle for sovereignty, or "Crisis" (Mekeel, 1943: p. 140). Some such period seems common, because it spans the transition from a "non-directed" situation in which neither of two societies in contact can or will coerce the other to a "directed" situation in which one (in our case, Euro-American) has clearly established and is using its dominance.

Marking the end of this second phase and the beginning of the third is some sort of agreement, usually a "Treaty" recording the surrender of sovereignty, which may be total, but more commonly involved only partial surrender. The degree of completeness of control marked by this was usually a reflection of the practical situation at the time of the treaty signing. If the thereafter dominant Euro-American society was represented by an overwhelming military or police presence, and was in a retributive mood after "repeated provocation," and if the native society was a battered remnant which had suffered many defeats, social dislocation, depopulation, and loss of leadership and cultural certainty, then the surrender was likely to be relatively complete, like that of Joseph's retreating Nez Percé in 1877 (McWhorter, 1952; Josephy, 1965). On the other hand, if the Anglo-Americans were very weakly represented, with little or no military potential or an ineffective force, and the Indian society in question was intact and undefeated, the treaty may have reserved substantial areas of aboriginal sovereignty like those negotiated in the mid-1850's throughout then Washington Territory by Governor Isaac I. Stevens who was supported by a very small force of troops, effectively no more than a guard detachment (Stevens, 1854; Manypenny, 1854, 1855; Haines, 1950).

The three main divisions of the sequence are: I. non-directed culture contact; II. overt culture conflict, ended by surrender of sovereignty; and III. directed culture contact. Having divided the sequence thus, I have made subsidiary divisions, to which we shall return. First, it is important to note that the sequence is presented in a way like that of Elkin's Australian sequence, as a flow-diagram in which one event leads to another with certain points at which choices, or different cultural strategies, are available. In addition, the two cultures are presented in columns with the initiators of contact, the Euro-Americans, in the first (left-hand) column, and the Indians in the second, as the society upon which pressures were brought in most cases. This follows Malinowski's suggestion for analyzing "European-Native" interaction in Africa (1945), but with emphasis on the effect on each society of what the other does or fails to do in a causally related manner, rather than on the specific institutions which result from these reactions. This sequence is therefore concerned with a diachronic analysis of intercultural reaction and an explanation of the mechanisms of such a dynamic relationship.

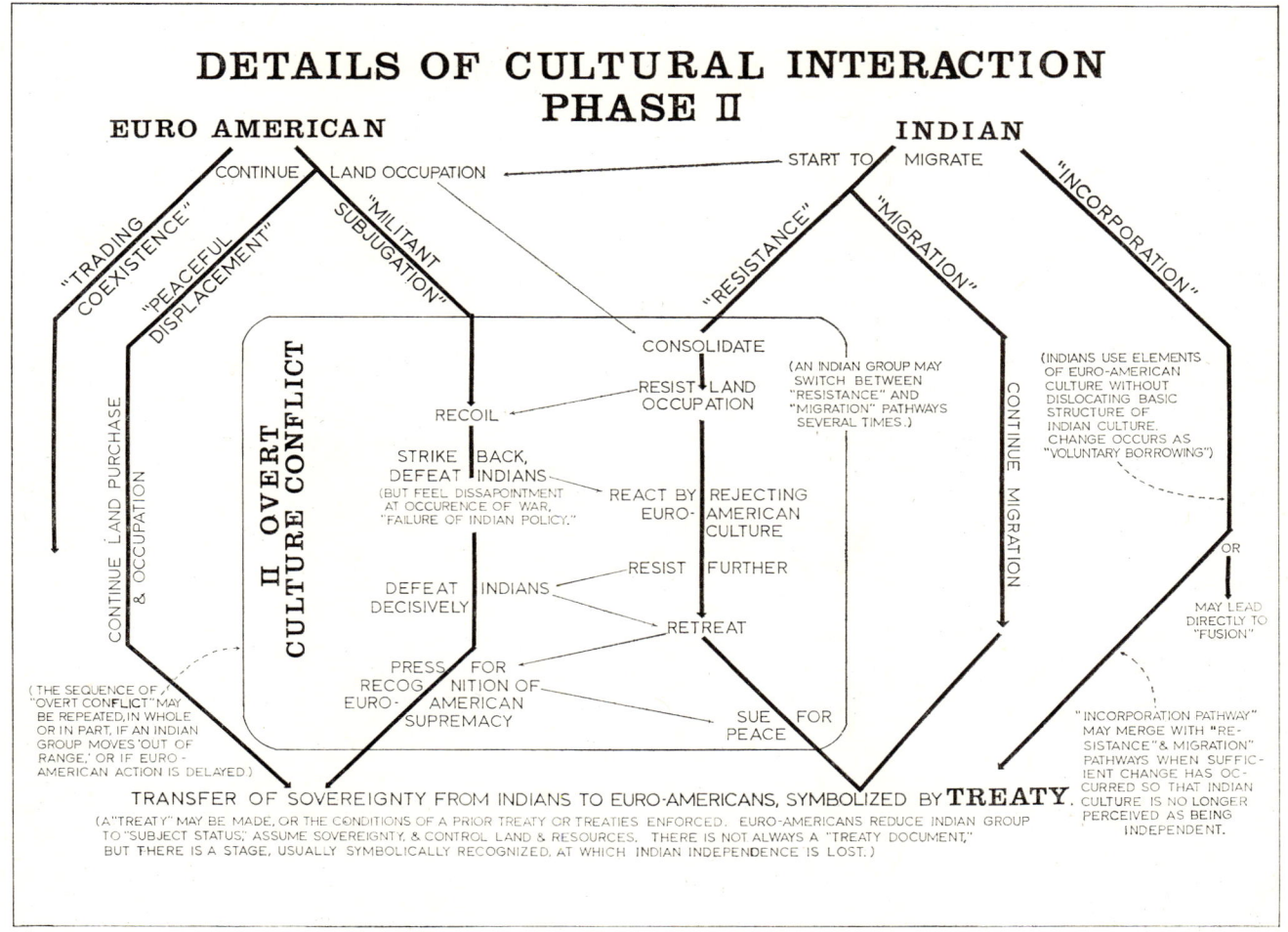

Fig. 4.

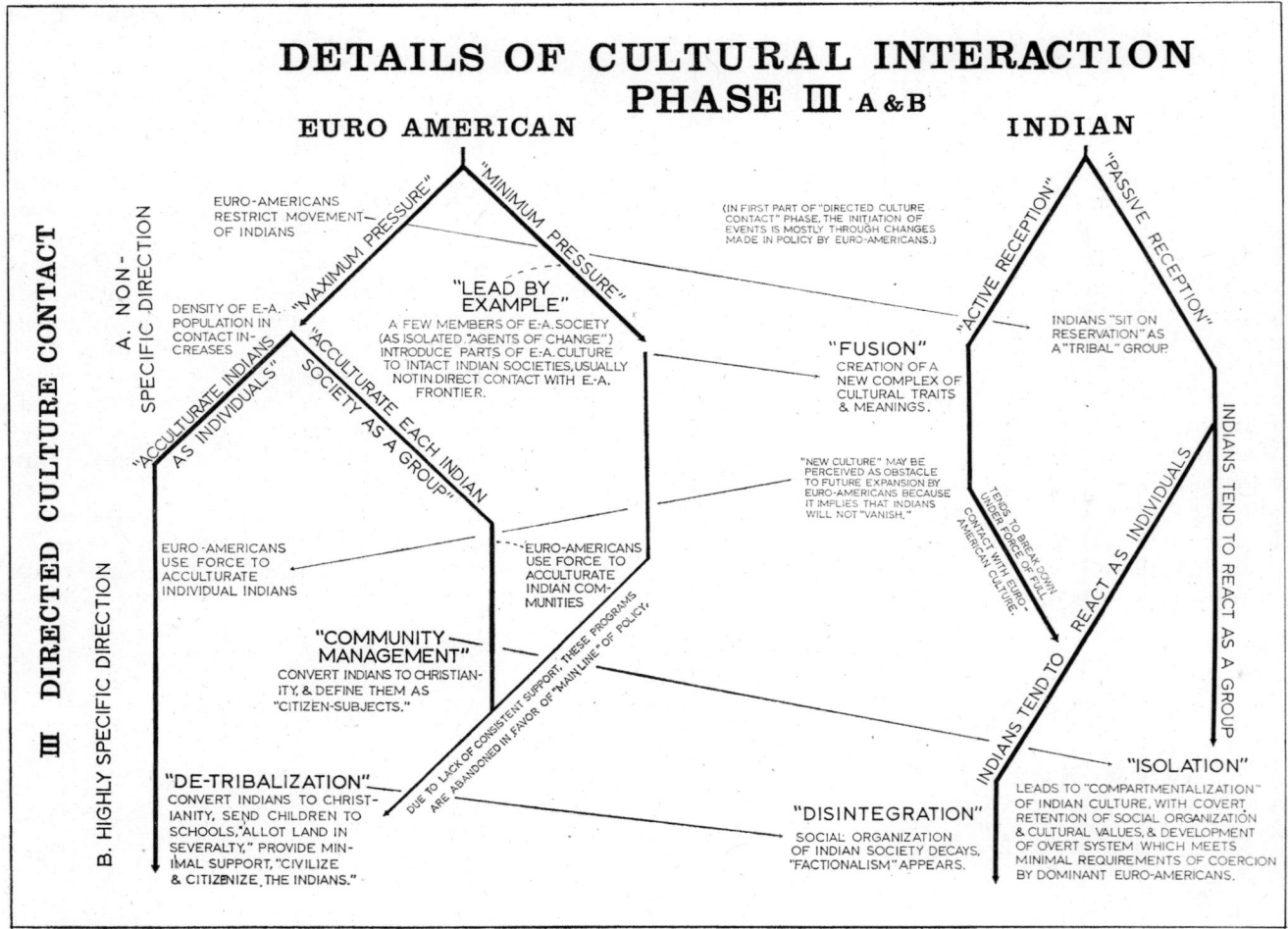

Fig. 5.

The subdivisions are considerably more arbitrary than the major divisions, and in some specific cases may occur together with each other, or not be readily distinguishable. The first major phase, "non-directed" contact, has been divided into a first subdivision of (A) "trade" and a second of (B) "land purchase." The difference may be expressed in terms of what the Indians were exchanging for material goods of Euro-American manufacture. Normally the two subphases occurred in the order (A) followed by (B), with the most common form of the first subphase being what we call "fur trade." However, in some cases in North America the two occurred together, and in cases where the Whites were not interested in whatever animal or vegetable resources the Indians might have to trade but only in land or mining resources (perhaps the gold rush in the northern Sierras would be an example), or where the Indians lived on a minimal subsistence economy with no surplus to trade (as in the western Great Basin) then only land was of interest, so that (A) "trade" was greatly reduced, and most of the first phase consisted of (B) "land purchase."

The "non-directed" phase can be considered at an end when Indians begin to feel coercive pressure from Anglo-Americans. Two basic choices were available—to fight or run. In most cases, the less powerful culture did both, but it should be noted that this second major phase, "overt culture conflict," was not inevitable. For example, the Flathead, some Shoshone, and some groups in California and in far western Canada and Alaska (excluding such people as the Haida and Nootka), never were in direct conflict. Thus it was possible to go directly from "non-directed" to "directed," with the transition compressed into land sales and the treaty which signified loss of Indian sovereignty. In fact, these two signifiers of the shift—loss of territory and loss of political self-determination—sometimes occurred as one. More commonly, however, the situation was as shown in the sequence, with some land cession preceding a period of crisis, and a surrender of native independence ending it.

Another variation occurred in cases where one or more treaties involving land and independence actually precipitated the period of crisis, which was finally ended by either enforcement of the terms of an earlier treaty, as in the case of the 1855 Walla Walla treaty which was definitively forced upon the Columbia Plateau Indians only after more than three years of fighting and negotiation (Larrabee, n.d., *a*), or by a new treaty which confirmed the victory of Euro-Americans, as the treaty of Greenville in 1795 validated the victory of General Wayne at Fallen Timbers (Prucha, 1962). One way or another, some official act usually signified the loss of freedom, and a period of crisis and physical resistance commonly preceded this. Finally, we should note again that there is no set period of time involved, and that the events of this second major phase were sometimes repeated several times, if the Indians in question could continue to migrate and avoid confinement and control by the Euro-Americans. Obvious examples occur among the Shawnee, Dakota, Navajo, and Apache, all of whom were able to move out of the range of European punitive action, sometimes for several generations.

Three subphases seem to be apparent in the last or "directed culture contact" phase, and again they form a series which may be repeated several times. I have characterized them as (A) "no specific direction," (b) "highly specific direction," and (C) "less specific direction," and they really signify rising and falling intensity of concern on the part of the superordinate culture toward the effort to direct change in the subordinate culture. In that sense, they reflect varying degrees to which this is a "directed" phase of culture contact. For example, it is clear that the period preceding passage of the Dawes Act of 1887 and during the first decades of its application was one of intense concern on the part of Anglo-Americans and of great pressure on Indians to incorporate White values.

This was followed by a reduction of interest leading to a disoriented nadir after World War I, the doldrums of Indian Policy, during which the dominant culture was unsure of its intentions. A new movement of concern arose in this relative vacuum (Downes, 1945; Philip, 1973). Special studies such as Schmeckebier's examination of the Bureau of Indian Affairs (1927) and the Merriam report (1928) on government Indian policy presaged the changes of the Collier administra-

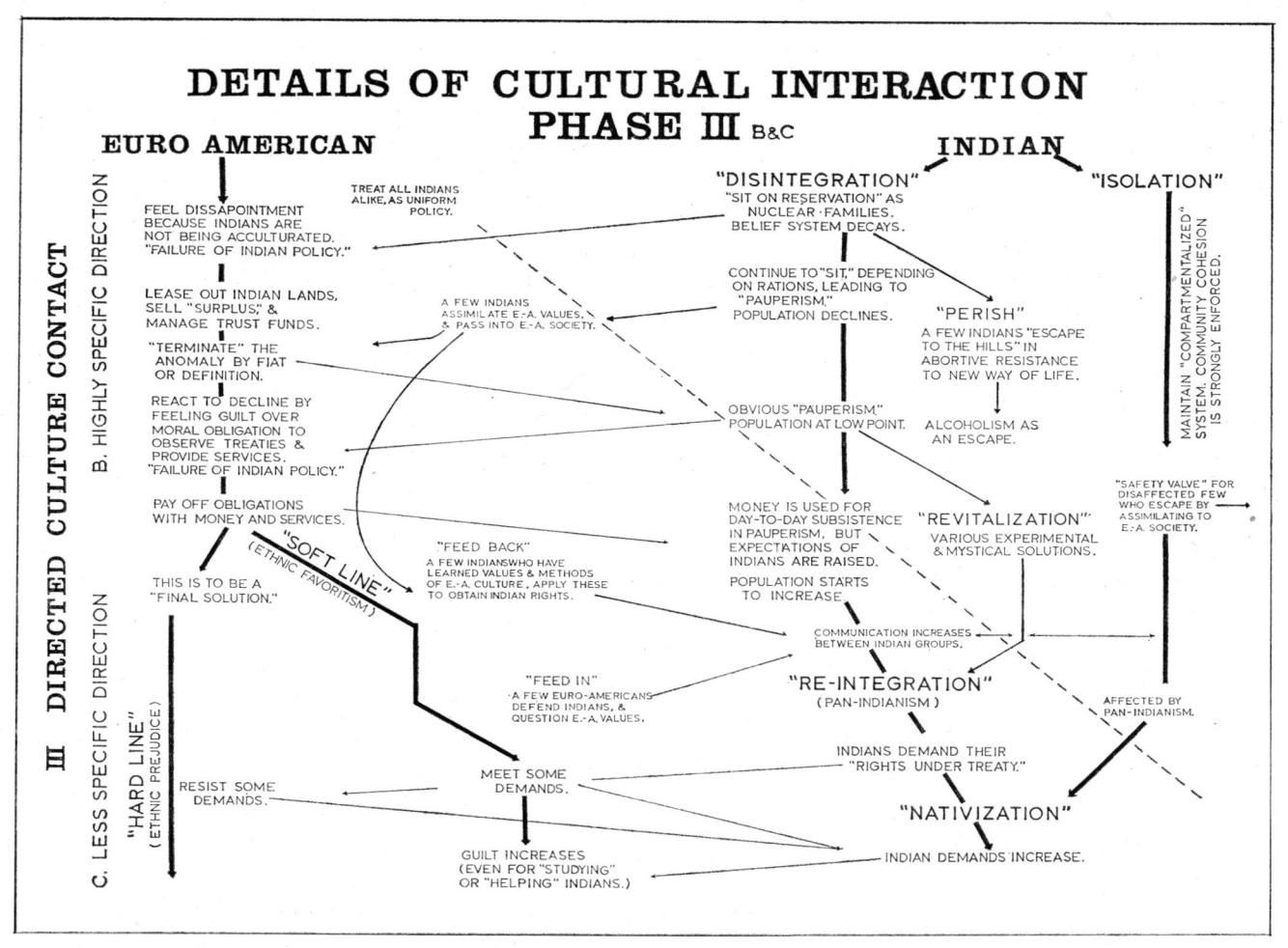

FIG. 6.

tion in the 1930's. Here was a new wave of interest, now phrased in terms of cultural pluralism, but involving the "democratization of tribal governments" to meet the requirements of the Indian Reorganization Act, and the enforcement of then current Euro-American concern with "erosion" of resources, to the extent of slaughtering thousands of Navajo sheep (Boyce, 1974), such that the Navajo felt that they had "submitted to conservation" imposed by an enthusiastic administration, rather than "achieved" a valuable condition on their own (Collier, 1947: p. 166). The Second World War and the "new normalcy" which followed it were marked by less interest in Indian Policy, but the spasmodic efforts at "Relocation" and "Termination" showed another upsurge. Again the attention of the superordinate society became less or was diverted elsewhere during the late 1950's and early 1960's, only to increase again with the wave of popular publication (Van Every, 1966; Steiner, 1968; Brown, 1970; DeLoria, 1967, 1973; Casteneda, 1968, 1971, 1973) and the revived ripple of "realistic" Indian movies at the end of the 1960's.

A listing of American commercial films with a point of view purported to be sympathetic to Indians shows these variations clearly:

Fort Apache	1947	*A Man Called Horse*	1970
Broken Arrow	1950	*Soldier Blue*	1970
Broken Lance	1954	*Little Big Man*	1970
Apache	1954	*Flap*	1970
Sitting Bull	1954	*When the Legends Die*	1970
The Searchers	1956	*The Man Who Loved Cat Dancing*	1970
Walk the Proud Land	1956	*Man in the Wilderness*	1971
Run of the Arrow	1957	*The Saga of Jeremiah Johnson*	1972
The Outsider	1961		
Cheyenne Autumn	1964		
Tell Them Willie Boy is Here	1969		

The films vary greatly in ethnographic detail, but they do show a tendency (perhaps cyclical or spiral since World War II) towards greater sympathy for the position of the Native North Americans involved. It will be noted that with two early exceptions, the first cluster of films showing interest was in the mid-1950's. This was followed by a pause, with the important exception of *Cheyenne Autumn*, and then the small flood of pictures referred to in 1969, 1970 and 1971. All these films have concerned themselves with the western half of North America, and with the exception of *The Outsider* (1961) and *Flap* and *When The Legends Die* (1970), they are not contemporary but are set in the "classic west" of mythology sometime in the latter third of the nineteenth century. The appearance of *Winterhawk* and *The Return of A Man Called Horse* in 1976 suggests that the cycle may be about to start again. The few depictions of culture contact in the east are almost all set during the frontier Indian wars of the third quarter of the eighteenth century, and were made some time ago.

Obvious examples are *Last of the Mohicans* (1936), *Drums Along the Mohawk* (1939), *Northwest Passage* (1940), and *Unconquered* (1947). In general they are clearly "unreconstructed" in their view of "red savagery." A somewhat more sympathetic view is *The Light in the Forest* (1958).

A phenomenon which is concurrent with the variations of interest by the directing society in superimposing its values is the growing acceptance, in part, of these values by the directed society which results in a pattern of variations in defensive concern that comes to be more and more directly an aspect of similar variation in the superordinate society, rather than a series of reactions to outside pressures. Thus, for example, during the Progressive Era before World War I a growing number of Indians became active in Anglo-American economic activities, joined or formed local "commercial clubs," and supported the optimistic, expansive, business-oriented world view which predominated in the superordinate culture (Olney, personal communication; Hertzberg, 1971). After that war, as some segments of Anglo-American culture placed emphasis on the worth of creative artisanship and handcrafts in opposition to standardized industrial mass production, various Indians, at first individually, then working with other members of their own respective societies, reasserted the value of their own traditional arts and successfully invented new forms of these (Marriot, 1948; LaFarge, 1940).

Similarly, the economic-political special interest pressure groups of the dominant society were mirrored in such institutions as the Native American Brotherhood (Drucker, 1958). The recent upsurge in activism, first expressed at meetings of Indian college students from various reservations, leading to "fish-ins" at Puyallup and culminating in the occupation of Alcatraz in 1969–1972, of the Washington, D. C., offices of the Bureau of Indian Affairs in November, 1972, and for seventy-one days at Wounded Knee (1972–1973), has many of the marks of similar activity on behalf of the civil rights movement during the 1960's and the subsequent protest against United States involvement in Southeast Asia. This even includes the shift from Ghandi-like passive resistance to the loss of "movement solidarity" and splinter-group violence which occurred in the larger culture.

In some senses, the "New Indian Activism," although working to "preserve the cultural heritage of Native Americans," and in many ways within various Indian cultural traditions (Lurie in: Leacock and Lurie, 1971), is also a sign of the success of four generations of Anglo-American agents of directed cultural change who have endeavored to bring the descendents of the pre-Columbian populations of North America into the dominant cultural system. It can be predicted that the fluctuations in concern will continue as long as a perceived cultural difference exists, but to some extent with the variations of interest among the Indians being part of variations in a larger, multi-ethnic American society, rather than solely reactions to acculturative pressures applied to them by the "directors of change" (White, 1974).

In examining the charts of sequential interaction, it is significant to note that there are several paired pathways, or cases where a particular course of action on the part of the Euro-Americans is matched by an appropriate reaction by the Indians with whom they are in contact—and sometimes *vice versa*. Thus, for example, a choice of "militant subjugation" on the part of Euro-Americans during the phase of Overt Culture Conflict is likely to be matched by "resistance" from the Native Americans, in contrast to which if the Euro-Americans choose "peaceful displacement" (as in the general policy of the colony of Pennsylvania in its early years) the Indians are more likely to match this with "migration." While this may seem self-evident, it is important to note that these "pairs" exist regardless of which party initiated the course of action.

In the Directed Culture Contact phase other "pairs" are Euro-American "minimum pressure" matched with "fusion" as a cultural alternative for Indians, Euro-American "maximum pressure" applied to a native community as a group paired with "isolation" as a tactic for that culture, and "maximum pressure" applied to assimilate Indians as individuals into the superordinate culture is associated with the "disintegration-reintegration" pathway for native American cultures. I have deliberately avoided saying that a particular action on the part of Euro-Americans causes a particular cultural result among Indians, even though it is clear that members of the dominant or superordinate culture are usually the initiators of change. The relationship is more complex than one of simple cause and effect, because the two or more interacting cultures have become part of larger systems of culture contact.

Another point of interest is the degree to which choices of cultural strategy are available. Not only may the superordinate and subordinate cultures choose various pathways at critical periods, but they can sometimes leave one track altogether and shift to another. This is possible only under certain conditions, and even the possibilities are limited. It will be useful to examine these in some detail.

During Non-Directed Culture Contact, either the contacting (Euro-American) or contacted (native American) culture may break off the contact, if there is room for maneuver, both geographically and socioeconomically. For example, a European colony, trading post, or mission may be destroyed or withdrawn, or an Indian group may move away from such a European establishment. This will not, of course, return either culture to the conditions in which it operated before contact, because various processes will have been started (changes in technology and social organization, for example) which do not simply disappear when the initial push stops, but it may make possible achievement of a new stability for one or both cultures.

More choices seem to be available in the Overt Culture Conflict phase. Here the Euro-Americans can change from "peaceful" to "militant" pathways and *vice versa,* doing this several times. Similarly, Indian groups may, as suggested earlier, "run or fight," or even move far enough away from pressure for long enough to go onto the "incorporative" pathway which is really outside the Overt Conflict relationship. All these choices however, are likely to lead both cultures ultimately to the symbolic "treaty" in which the dominant position of the Euro-American is officially expressed.

When there is specific direction of the subordinate culture by the dominant one, there are still a number of strategies available. This is true not only for the individuals who act as agents of change in subordinate groups, which in this sense may now be considered as ethnic enclaves or minority communities within the superordinate society (Barth, 1969: p. 33), but also for various members of the dominant culture, such as John Collier or Oliver LaFarge (Collier, 1947; Philip, 1973; McNickle, 1971). On the charts, I have characterized the direction of those Euro-Americans who came to advocate permissive attitudes (i.e., tolerant of cultural pluralism and diversity) as the "soft line," marked by more guilt than that felt by other members of the superordinate society, more compelled by treaty and other obligations, and more subject to social conscience and "ethnic favoritism." Those who continued to push for full acceptance of Euro-American values as the only correct course for individuals of Native American background I have placed in the "hard line" of continuing directed culture contact, characterized by overt ethnocentrism or ethnic prejudice. A good example would be Senator Watkins in the debate over "Termination" (Watkins, 1957; LaFarge, 1957). "Soft line" in this context is not quite the same as the concept put forward by Jorgenson (in Waddell and Watson, 1971, and 1972) and Aberle (1973) of Whites pressuring Indians to "organize as corporate entities" (Aberle, 1973: p. 70), but it is certainly related, and the "hard line" may be equated with the frequently noted "Protestant-ethic individualism."

A point of particular interest is that there seem to have been more major pathways and subsidiary paths utilized by the native cultures than by the Euro-Americans. This may reflect a curious phenomenon—that the dominant culture is usually the initiator of action, but then becomes locked into one of a few courses of action, while the subordinate cultures are more free to experiment. One reason might be because there is less cause to question basic values among members of an apparently successful society than among members of a subordinate one. It may also simply be a manifestation of desperate seeking after cultural and personal survival, amelioration of discomfort, and salvation by Indians. They have tried many more cultural strategies than the White man because they had to.

USES OF THE MODEL

If this graphic representation is to have explanatory value, it must meet two requirements. The first is that a particular relationship of a specific Amerindian culture and some form of the broad cultural grouping we have called Euro-American (e.g., the Yaqui relationship with Jesuit-Spanish-Mexican, or the western Unami Delaware relationship with Quaker Pennsylvania—early federal United States) can be traced on it. The pathways taken by the Yaqui, for example, involved nearly a century (Spicer's "Rancheria Phase," in Spicer *et al.*, 1961) of movement through "cultural augmentation" and "incorporation" routes directly to "fusion," bypassing any surrender of sovereignty under "treaty." This next phase (Spicer's "mission," and part of "autonomous") then lasted for a century and a half, until after the expulsion of the Jesuits from New Spain, and into a stage of complete cultural independence from Hispanic Mexico, which later became a military struggle that ended with Sonoran-Mexican conquest in the late nineteenth century. In other words, having bypassed the loss of sovereignty by going directly to fusion, the Yaqui relationship with Hispano-Mexicans later reverted to Phase II, "conflict," after which the Yaqui found themselves on a route through defeat, "treaty," and individual reaction on the "Disintegration-reintegration" pathway. This had been perceived as the road to "assimilation" by the 1956 symposium (Spicer *et al.*, 1961), but I think two additional decades of Indian-White relations have made it clear that cultural and social disintegration have been, and are being, followed by reintegration in the case of most Native North American societies which survived the stage of maximum stress. Assimilation is a side route or escape taken by a few Indians on the "disintegration-reintegration" pathway, and by a few escaping the extreme pressures for conformity on the "isolation" pathway, but, although assimilation was the stated goal of much Euro-American policy under "highly specific directed culture contact," it does not seem to be the result for Indian cultures under this pressure (Schlesier, 1974).

In the case of the Delaware (Newcomb, 1956) we can trace the route of the main body, which was contacted in the early seventeenth century, started to migrate later in that century, threw off Iroquois domination, and moved to overt conflict with Anglo-Americans in the 1750's, and alternated resistance (until 1811) and migration until the mid-nineteenth century, when remnants were settled in the mid-West, and after the Civil War in Oklahoma. There they underwent social disintegration during the end of the nineteenth century and first half of the twentieth, by now as part of an increasingly amalgamated body of Indians from different societies who were reacting to uniform application of United States government policies. Several currents of "revitalization" can be seen (most notably the Native American Church) which precede involvement in the larger Pan-Indian movement (Weslager, 1972).

The Brotherton band, whose experiences prompted this effort to create a working *schema* for describing Indian-White relations, took a somewhat variant route up to the nineteenth century. They shared the common movement of the Unami Lenape until about 1745, but continued migrating (in this case on a small geographic scale, and to locations behind the Anglo-American frontier of settlement, rather than west of and beyond it) and scrupulously avoided the "resistance" pathway. Both the direction of movement and the avoidance of conflict suggest that this group preferred Anglo-American control to that of the Iroquois or the newly emergent political leaders of other Delaware. The year 1758 clearly marks a recognized transfer of sovereignty by treaty, and for about a decade after that the scanty evidence suggests that Brotherton was a community under relatively little coercive acculturative pressure, where "fusion" was taking place. This collapsed because of lack of interest and support by the surrounding New Jersey colonists, and by 1771 the people of Brotherton were on a "disintegrative" route to which the province and state reacted with policy strikingly like the United States federal government's Indian policy a century later. By 1802 the Brotherton band was in a condition of "pauperism," and the state of New Jersey "terminated" the community. However, there was a marked difference between the options available as strategies of cultural survival for Brotherton Delawares in 1802 and for the general population of reservation Indians in the United States in the early twentieth century. The latter had no place to go, but the Brotherton band could still move, and did so, first to upstate New York and then to Wisconsin. By 1822 they had joined the main body of Unami, which was in the process of dividing into different communities, and from the mid-nineteenth century on the descendants of people originally living at Brotherton were merged with other Delawares and moved along a "disintegration-reintegration" pathway similar to that taken by their ancestors a century earlier, but this time without the escape route of further migration.

Events at Brotherton resemble a much larger pattern of cultural contact relationship in North America. The reason for this resemblance, and, in fact, for the patterning itself, is that we are seeing the result of the repeated interaction of underlying cultural themes. Not only are themes in varying Indian cultures and themes in Euro-American culture present, and reacting upon each other, but an intercultural relationship has come into existence and developed over some dozen human generations. This relationship has developed its own dynamic logic, and its own themes. In Section VI I shall discuss these fundamental emphases of the various systems starting with those common to, or frequently ascribed to, the Indians, then those shared between Indian and Euro-American, those underlying Euro-American beliefs, and finally those which I feel have developed as part of the changing relationship between cultures in North America.

The first requirement of the model of North American cultural interaction is that various specific sequences like the three examples above can be fitted into it. It serves to chart the various routes which were taken by different parts of Euro-American culture and by what is now an increasingly unified Native North American culture. Other particular ethno-historical sequences north of Mexico can also be fitted without much difficulty. They will differ from each other, but many of them will follow a fairly straightforward route through "resistance" and/or "migration" to 'treaty,' and down the socially atomistic "disintegration-reintegration" path. This is the typical route for most aboriginal societies north of Mexico, but considerable variation is possible, especially in the western and northern areas.

I think the reason that members of the 1956 symposium (Spicer et al., 1961: p. 541) did not think such patterning was probable was because, among the six cultures they considered, only one (the Mandan) was east of the Rocky Mountains. The Yaqui presented a very strong example of "fusion" (as do the Cherokee; Gearing, 1962), the Pueblos of "isolation," and the Navajo of "incorporation." The remaining two groups were Wishram (marginal Columbia Plateau) and Kwakiutl (with highly developed Northwest Coast culture), and both presented certain values in aboriginal state which were coincident with values pressed upon them by the superordinate Anglo-Americans, so that the effects of acculturative pressure were, in a sense, not so disruptive of the native world view. All six of these cultures can be fitted into the sequence, but only the Mandan are in the typical pattern. The most common route for Indian-White relations north of the Rio Grande was that established and repeated, with variations, in the eastern two-thirds of the continent, from the St. Lawrence valley south to the Gulf of Mexico. Only one of the six ethno-histories of culture contact considered in 1956 was in that area, so that members of the symposium (Spicer, Dozier, Bruner, Vogt, French, and Codere), although they are responsible for identifying and defining most possible pathways of the present model, did not perceive them as related parts of an overall sequence.

The second major requirement of the model is that it must not only adequately describe, but must explain. It does this through two major mechanisms, both of which produced a sequence which, as a whole, is causal. The first is the device of showing a constant back-and-forth flow of influence (this is brought out on the four charts of "details of cultural interaction"), so that changes in attitude or of options available for Indians can be understood in terms of Euro-American actions, but equally so that Euro-American perceptions and beliefs are seen in relation to the role of the Indians at that time. By this means, it can be seen that even so apparently powerless, passive, and negative an action by Indians as simply continuing to exist in a state of cultural difference and economic poverty can shape the reaction of members of the dominant society. No one move by one culture is a simple, complete cause of an inevitable reaction on the part of the other, because each is moving in terms of its own ecological adaptation, its own value system, its past experiences, its social organization, and its population dynamics. However, the action (or even inaction) of one culture in an interrelationship of the sort shown in this model is certainly a vitally important input for shaping the options available to, and probable preferred choice of, the other culture.

The other major mechanism involves the cultural themes discussed earlier in this paper, including themes which have developed and become part of the on-going relationship. Just as the shared theme which perceived the Indians as "vanishing" colored much of the latter eighteenth- and all of the nineteenth-century periods of the larger relationship, so it appears that a shared theme which perceives Indians as "wronged" is becoming a dominant aspect of that relationship now. An equally important use of themes has been identifying deep foundations for belief and value systems which in some cases create underlying instabilities in the cultures involved. The conflicts within Euro-American culture between a sense of guilt and obligation and a hard belief in the rightness of our system of work, property, and interpersonal responsibility is a case in point. Further analysis of these themes appears in the subsequent conclusion to this paper. Taken together, the two forces of constant feedback of action between cultures and conflict between themes of different cultures, among themes of one culture, and even conflict caused by shared themes, have provided the motion along the various pathways of this sequence.

VI. ANALYSIS OF INTERACTION OF CULTURAL THEMES

THEMES COMMON TO NATIVE NORTH AMERICAN CULTURES

There is no question that profound differences existed between the entities defined by ethnographic research as the separate cultures of North America. Those differences were great even between the cognitive systems of societies within each of the arbitrary categorizing constructs we call "Culture Areas," and were even more pronounced between groups in different areas. What cultural themes then did they have in common? The answer lies partly in a basic fact of cultural ecology—most North American Indian societies, including even the intensive horticulturalists of the southeastern river valleys, relied at least partly on hunting and gathering for subsistence. In some cases this reliance was relatively minor in terms of the proportion of food produced or output of energy, but even in these cases it received considerable cultural emphasis. Combined with this was the use of one or another sort of kin-based group as the primary focus of social organization and membership, the stressing of an individual's obligations to this group at the expense of his own personal interests, and the attribution of considerable importance to the free will and desires of each person by all others in his group. The seeming contradiction in these last two occurs only because of the meaning Euro-American culture puts on individualism. Perhaps we can summarize the pertinent themes which seem common to many Native North American cultures as follows: a man should be a hunter-warrior; a woman should be a gatherer-gardener; a person should be responsible to his kin group; one should avoid hurting others in his kin group even at cost to himself—one should "be generous"; no person should be coerced and if possible his desires should be met.

Another factor which increased the similarity between the fundamental assumptions of differing Indian cultures was that initial contact with the complex and rich material culture of Euro-Americans tended to produce similar effects. For example, both those aboriginal cultures with elaborate ceramic techniques and those with no pottery at all tended to welcome the addition of the iron or copper cooking kettle. This effect was particularly pronounced in the categories of male hunting and fighting tools and weapons and in fabrics. Because these trading contacts made different Native North American societies behave alike toward the Euro-Americans and their goods, they increased the visible similarities between the varying cultures, as viewed by the Euro-Americans.

A final and most important point concerns precisely this visibility. There has been a strong tendency on the part of Euro-Americans, whose stress has historically been on farming-fortune seeking, to perceive all the different cultures with which they came in contact as being alike. Thus the emphasis of the Indian man on being a hunter-warrior has been magnified in Euro-American eyes by the similar effects on different aboriginal cultures of contact with Whites, and then magnified again by the Euro-American assumption that a man's proper role was that of an acquisitive farmer. If these Indian men were different from Euro-American men, if they deviated from what was natural, proper, and normal behavior, and if they all did some hunting, then they all came to be defined, by contrast with the "civilized" White farmer, as "savage hunters." The profound differences between one Indian society and another were largely ignored by the Euro-Americans in favor of the single fact of difference between their own complex "civilization" and the simple "savagery" of all Indians, lumped together. In other words, there are in fact some themes shared by varying Indian cultures as a result of their similar ecological adaptations, and there is also the ascription to them of even greater uniformity by Euro-Americans who were unable to see the different values that did exist.

THEMES COINCIDENT TO INDIAN AND EURO-AMERICAN CULTURES

The problem here was that those values which fell into this common ground were usually not really identical in meaning. Consequently, the apparent area of shared interest was somewhat smaller in reality than as perceived from either culture. This factor, which made the shared area deceptively larger than it actually was, meant that often the Euro-Americans and the Indians were talking at cross-purposes when they seemed to be using equivalent terms in dealing with each other. For example, both agreed that a friendly or peaceful relationship should ideally be maintained, but the interpretation was different. To the Whites, this meant that the Indians would be quiet, cause no trouble, and be in general subservient to the wishes of the government. To the Native North Americans, the same phrase at a treaty conference meant that their group would be treated with proper dignity and as equals, and that if disputes arose (which might even include the possibility of occasional violence), they would be settled through appropriate channels of inter-societal diplomacy. A basic psychological difference existed between the Euro-Americans, who wanted a chief's signature at the bottom line of a treaty, and the Indians, who wanted the symbolic performance of treaty diplomacy (Kardas, personal communication). The Whites would go through with what they considered savage foolishness in order to obtain an agreement they could feel was legally binding, and the natives were willing to put a mark on a piece of paper in order to have the all-important conference. Here the seeming agreement about a friendly relationship masked a contradiction between the end-oriented document emphasis of the Euro-Americans and the means-oriented ceremonial emphasis of the Indians.

Similarly, the ideal of economic self-sufficiency for the reservation group has had very different interpretations, since to the Euro-American it meant that the Indians should become profit-seeking extensive field farmers, like themselves, each nuclear family producing and selling a surplus of foodstuffs, while the Indians usually expected to reap some benefits of the White man's technology of food production and still maintain their own pattern of environmental resource utilization.

THEMES COMMON TO EURO-AMERICAN CULTURE

Strong cultural emphases of Anglo-American colonists have, like those of the Indians and those shared, already been presented. Just as there were differences between different aboriginal cultures, so were there differences between the belief and behavior systems of the incoming Europeans. Certain major themes, however, were common to all Europeans, and when contrasted with Native North American cultural emphases, the differences among Europeans of different nations are less important than their similarities. These themes most important for this discussion may be put forth as follows:

A man should be a husbander-exploiter (in eighteenth-century terms, a yeoman farmer).

A woman should be a mother and housekeeper.

A man should work to improve his social and economic standing competitively, on his own land. He should seek his fortune, but not too single-mindedly.

All land and all resources associated with it should be owned by some one (who should "work it" to "use it").

A person should feel guilty about certain long-standing social situations which do not meet the stated ideals of the culture. This is especially true where the weak have been defeated by the strong.

It is true that the outward form by means of which some of these themes are expressed has changed over several centuries, but this had not affected the underlying value. The normal role of the Euro-American male at present, for instance, involves activities in manufacturing or commerce much more often than it does farming, but the business with which a man is concerned or for which he works, or the union to which he belongs, is still supposed to grow in size, to prosper with increasing profits from investment of capital and labor, just as the ideal successful farm of one or two centuries ago was supposed to behave. What is most significant is that these core-values concerning roles and expectation of personal success in Euro-American culture have not changed significantly in some three or four centuries. The specific form of the role of a man has changed from agriculture to business, but his generalized role has consistently been that of one who husbands his resources in order to invest them for personal profit in the exploitation of his surroundings. "Underutilized skills," "low productivity," "capital not invested," or "resources not developed" have the same opprobrium attached to them now that "land lying unused" did in the eighteenth or nineteenth century. Current examples of the application of this theme to Native North American cultures are the "economic development" of the Hopi lands at Black Mesa, and the enormous pressures for equivalent uses of lands assigned under the Alaska Native Claims Settlement Act of 1971 (Harrison, 1972). For one interpretation of this theme as an example of the way in which marginal areas are exploited to support the growing power center of Euro-American culture, see Jorgenson's suggestive study of the Northern Utes (in Wadell and Watson, 1971), and of the Sun Dance among the Shoshone (1972).

THEMES WHICH HAVE EMERGED AS THE INTERCULTURAL RELATIONSHIP DEVELOPED

There are several identifiable focuses of the relationship itself. The first concerns the aboriginal cultures and the next two the Euro-American. In all cases of contact between Indian and Euro-American cultures, with the exception of a few of the earliest eastern-seaboard colonization attempts, the Indian cultures were less powerful, and were placed in a subordinate position by the treaty-making process, and throughout the Directed Culture Contact phase. Usually the relative differential in power was at least partially apparent even before Indian sovereignty was lost, and it was certainly clearly spelled out after that had occurred. Under these circumstances, it seems that it is common for the subordinate society to react more profoundly than the more powerful or superordinate society.

It should be noted that there is some recent evidence to suggest that this predominantly one-way phenomenon may be true at the beginning of Directed Culture Contact, and for a long time thereafter, but may eventually be modified as the dominant or superordinate society begins to be increasingly affected by either the specific values of a subordinate society (Hallowell, 1957), or by the very continued existence of such societies and by the prolongation of the dominant-subordinate relationship. This may be the result of growing doubt and disappointment as expectations of rapid assimilation of the Indian cultures in the mainstream of Euro-American culture have not been met. It is also possible that the increasing amount by which Euro-American culture is being influenced by various Indian cultures (or by pan-Indian culture) actually reflects a shift in power, that is, a lessening of the degree to which Euro-American society is superordinate and the Indian societies, individually or collectively, subordinate.

In any event, for most of the sequence under consideration, the subordinate society has been more affected by contact than the superordinate. There are four major reasons for this. First we must consider demographic and economic adaptation to the environment, because the two go together in the case of cultures in contact. The population of a group which has previously had contact only with neighboring groups does not normally have the resistance to a broad spectrum of diseases that a more cosmopolitan population does. This effect is magnified when whole continents have been isolated for millennia from the rest of the humanity, so that widespread mortality is the result of the introduction of diseases new to the relatively isolated natives of the Americas. In addition, as trade, land sales, migration, and sometimes overt conflict develop, that part of the population which has survived new diseases is simultaneously subject to a variety of disruptions and dislocations, few of which are likely to produce the stability of social organization and prospect of future tranquility and plenty which lead to maintenance of the size of the population. Thus, the number of people in a contacted society is almost always going to decrease, and certainly the pre-contact economic system will be profoundly altered by this change in population size (Codere, 1950). In addition, the economic and subsistence base will have been disrupted by the increasing demand for and dependence on the manufactured goods of the more technologically complex culture (Sharp, 1952).

A second area in which the subordinate culture will be more upset than the superordinate is that of basic values. These are shaken by the introduction of the new goods, by the various epidemic diseases and high death rate, by the inability to defeat, or even stop for long, the superordinate culture if open conflict occurs. The more the power differential widens between the two cultures, the more the belief system which explained and justified the previous perception of the universe will be felt inadequate.

The third reason for greater disruption of the aboriginal culture follows from this same growing discrepancy in power. Neither the normal (i.e., customary) nor abnormal (some innovative, some merely desperate) reactions from pre-contact times seem to solve the situation. The old systems fail, and it is not surprising that a series of new solutions are then tried, but that none of them affects the power relationship (Jorgenson, 1972; Mooney, 1965). Some may provide some personal satisfaction, and this seems to be the source of strength of many revitalization movements, but the more these digress from the aboriginal beliefs and practices, the more the subordinate culture changes in reaction to pressures (A. F. C. Wallace, 1969; French, 1948).

Finally, as the relationship becomes more and more one of Directed Culture Contact, the dominant society is in a position to try to work its will on the subordinate one. The result may not be what the official agents of change in the superordinate culture intend, but the ability to exert this kind of pressure inevitably does produce marked change in the receiving culture. And, of course, the very fact of being in a position to be manipulated, combined with the failure of either customary or innovative solutions to solve the crisis or remove the pressure, proves to the members of the subordinate society that their culture is in an inferior position. This leads to further doubt of the old values, and to continued change.

Two of the major focuses or themes which have developed out of on-going North American culture contact have more to do with Euro-American than with Indian cultures. These themes concern first the fact that normally the dominant culture simply assumes its own superiority, and second, the consequences for the relationship when that "natural superiority and moral right" is questioned from within.

It is no great surprise to discover that the cultural victories of the more powerful society soon become self-justifying. Time and again the proof was tangibly presented to the Euro-Americans that the supremacy of "civilization" over "savagery" was inevitable, pre-ordained by Providence, and a proof of the moral superiority of Euro-American civilization (Pearce, 1953, 1957; Smith, 1950). Indians "melted away" at first contact, sometimes even in the generation or two before, as diseases moved ahead of exploration. Those that remained seemed demoralized, and many even appeared to welcome the incoming culture. A few resisted, with "barbarous" methods of course, and were invariably defeated after they had achieved a few initial successes only by their use of "cowardly tactics" to attack "defenseless noncombatants." Given the many repetitions of Indian defeat, demoralization, and disappearance, it is no wonder that members of the superordinate society did not question their own superiority or their moral right to overcome, although some of them might question the means.

Another reason that the values of the dominant culture were not immediately challenged is that the Euro-Americans' culture itself was intact and thriving. There is just no reason to challenge one's own fundamental assumptions on the basis of contact with an "obviously inferior" (i.e., less powerful) society. To do so is to threaten one's own world view, self conception, and identity without cause, since the evidence in front of one seems to validate these beliefs repeatedly. Very few members of the dominant culture were motivated to do this, and those few were marginal members of their society, like the frontier trappers who became the "mountain men" of the early nineteenth century. It is interesting to note this effect of culture contact: when the power differential is considerable, the values of the superordinate culture tend to be supported, or even intensified, by contrast with the "self-evident" inferiority of the subordinate culture.

A good spokesman for this unquestioning view of the superiority of Euro-American civilization was F. J. Turner in his best-known writings. The frontier perceived by Turner's pioneers was essentially an empty one, the development or civilizing of which was supposed to produce various liberating effects on those who took part in the process. It is not surprising that this late nineteenth-century view of the effect of the frontier on Euro-American culture in the United States simply did not perceive the land to have been occupied or used in any meaningful way prior to the arrival of the pioneer farmer. From this point of view the Indian had been a fleeting presence who disappeared during the period of the frontiersman, the half-savage and necessarily sacrificed cutting edge of "civilization," the Natty Bumpos and Daniel Boones and Tom Quicks of fiction and local legend, who "made the land safe" for the true Americans, the pioneer farmers who followed them (Smith, 1950; Pearce, 1953, 1957; Bevier, 1846; Bross, 1887; Crumb, 1936; Gardiner, 1888; Quinlan, 1851).

This is not to say that there were not some changes or developments in Euro-American culture as a result of some ten generations of expansion into land not previously occupied by a dense-population, complex-technology, extensive-field-farming, stratified society. There were, and it was to these (or to an idealized version of them) that Turner addressed himself, but he was not writing about culture contact, because it did not significantly alter the values of his own culture, at least not as part of the phenomenon he was examining (Billington, 1967; Webb, 1952; Taylor, 1956).

Despite the overriding assumption of self-proven superiority, increasingly there have been doubts raised by Euro-Americans in action and thought. They have questioned the means by which their society has become superordinate, what it has done in that position, and even some of their own values. It is this growing tension within the dominant culture which constitutes the second major theme concerned with Euro-Americans during the last several centuries of culture contact. This internal conflict of values has occurred in two forms, the first of which is represented by the contrast between the frequent official insistence on observation of the legal niceties of agreements with Indian groups, as opposed to the impatient and occasionally lawless acts of frontier settlers. The second in effect pivots in the other direction from the same center. Here the official policy of the Euro-American society is challenged, not by the illegal violence of frontier "Indian haters," but by insistence that treaties and laws should be interpreted in their most literal sense so as to give the benefit of any judgment to the disadvantaged or minority group, that is, to the Indians. In other words, this conflict is between the official position (which I have earlier here called "the hard line") of Euro-American society that other cultural groups should become like us (that is, be assimilated), and the "Indian lovers" (or "soft liners") who have increasingly doubted both the practical wisdom and the ethical propriety of enforcing cultural uniformity. These people have rarely gone so far as to challenge overtly the fact of directing which is inherent to a Directed Culture-Contact situation, but they have often attacked the form and objectives of the direction which has occurred, and urged reform of "Indian policy."

It is a gross oversimplification and a misapplication of modern politically charged phrases to characterize these two internal conflicts as representing extreme right- and left-wing assaults on the main line core values of Euro-American culture, but there is some truth to the analogy. The effect of these challenges, from either extreme, has been to produce fluctuations in the direction of official policy, and alternations in the degree of acculturative pressure applied to different aboriginal groups at different times. Even the few attempts at wholesale or blanket application of policy directives have, in fact, been of greatly varying intensity. The General Allotment Act of 1887 was widely applied to the plains Indians, but other important groups, and whole culture areas such as the northeastern woodlands (various Pennsylvania and New York Iroquois, for example) and the desert southwest were scarcely affected. In 1934 the Indian Reorganization bill called for a completely new approach to Indian Policy (Collier, 1947: pp. 154–171), but was rejected on a number of reservations, including the largest one—the Navajo. Another policy change in the early 1950's called for termination of the federal responsibility, but this complete withdrawal of trusteeship was suffered by only a few groups (the Menominee and Klamath are the best examples—Zimmerman, 1957; LaFarge, 1957; Watkins, 1957). A similar situation has applied in Canada (McNickle, 1973). Despite occasional noises in the direction of logical consistency, Euro-American society apparently is too complex, with too many conflicting themes, to play a monolithic role in a culture-contact situation. This is not to say that the overwhelming power of this superordinate culture has not had profound effects on the native cultures of North America—only that the direction and intensity of application of that power have fluctuated so greatly as to produce a variety of different effects, a variety reflected in alternate pathways of Indian cultural response.

BIBLIOGRAPHY

ABERLE, DAVID P. 1973. "The Sun Dance and Reservation Underdevelopment." (Review of Joseph Jorgenson's *The Sun Dance Religion: Power for the Powerless.* [Chicago, University of Chicago Press, 1972]) *Journal of Ethnic Studies* 1, 2: pp. 66–73.

ACRELIUS, ISRAEL. 1876. *A History of New Sweden: or, the Settlements on the River Delaware.* (Translated from the Swedish with introduction and notes by W. M. Reynolds.) *Memoirs of the Historical Society of Pennsylvania* 2.

ALLINSON, SAMUEL. 1776. *Acts of the General Assembly of the Province of New Jersey from . . . 1702 . . . to . . . 1776* (Burlington, N.J., Isaac Collins, Printer).

ALLINSON, SAMUEL (2nd). 1875. "A Fragmentary History of New Jersey Indians." New Jersey Hist. Soc. *Proc.* (ser. 2) 4: pp. 34–50.

BARBER, JOHN W., and HENRY HOWE. 1844. *Historical Collections of the State of New Jersey* (New York, S. Tuttle).

BARTH, FREDRIK, editor. 1969. *Ethnic Groups and Boundaries* (Boston, Little, Brown & Co.).

BERKHOFER, ROBERT F., JR. 1963. "Protestants, Pagans, and Sequences among the North American Indians, 1760–1860." *Ethnohistory* 10: pp. 201–216.

BEVIER, ABRAHAM GARRET. 1846. *The Indians: or Narratives of Massacres and Depredations on the Frontier in Wawasink and its Vicinity during the American Revolution* (Roundout, N.Y.).

BILLINGTON, RAY ALLEN. 1967. "The American Frontier." Chapter 1 in: Paul Bohannen and Fred Plog, editors, *Beyond the Frontier* (New York, Natural History Press), pp. 3–24.

BISBEE, HENRY H. 1971. *Sign Posts, Place Names in History of Burlington County, New Jersey* (Willingboro, N.J., Alexia Press).

BOYCE, GEORGE A. 1974. *When Navajos Had too Many Sheep: the 1940's* (San Francisco, Indian Historian Press).

BRAINERD, DAVID. 1745. Letter to Reverend John Sergeant, Princeton University MS. Collections.

BRAINERD, JOHN. n.d. "John Brainerd Papers." Princeton University MS. Collections.

—— 1761–1762. "Journal." Princeton University MS. Collections.

—— 1880. "The Journal of the Rev. John Brainerd from January, 1761, to October, 1762." Introduction by Prof. George Macloskie, L.L.D. (Toms River, N.J., the New Jersey *Courier*).

BRAINERD, JONATHAN. 1884. *Memoirs of Reverend David Brainerd, Based on the Life of Brainerd Prepared by Jonathan Edwards, D.D., and Afterwards Revised and enlarged by S. E. Dwight* (New York).

BRAINERD, THOMAS. 1865. *The Life of John Brainerd, the Brother of David Brainerd and His Successor as Missionary to the Indians of New Jersey.* (Philadelphia, the Presbyterian Publication Committee).

BROSS, WILLIAM. 1887. *Legend of the Delaware: An Historical Sketch of Tom Quick to Which is Added the Winfield Family* (Chicago).

BROWN, DEE. 1970. *Bury My Heart at Wounded Knee* (New York, Bantam Books).

CASTENEDA, CARLOS. 1968. *The Teachings of Don Juan, A Yaqui Way of Knowledge* (New York, Ballantine Books).

—— 1971. *A Separate Reality: Further Conversations with Don Juan* (New York, Simon and Schuster).

CHAGNON, NAPOLEON A. 1968. *Yanomamö: The Fierce People* (New York, Holt Rinehart & Winston).

Cherokee Nation v. State of Georgia. 1831.

CODERE, HELEN. 1950. *Fighting With Property, A Study of Kwakiutl Potlatching and Warfare, 1792–1930* (Seattle, University of Washington Press).

COHEN, FELIX. 1942. *Handbook of Federal Indian Law* (Washington, D.C., U.S. Government Printing Office).

COLLIER, JOHN. 1947. *Indians of the Americas, The Long Hope* (abridged, New York, Mentor Books).

COSTO, RUPERT. 1970. "Alcatraz." *The Indian Historian* 3, 1: pp. 4–12, 64.

CRUMB, FRED W. 1936. *Tom Quick, Early American* (Narrowsburg, N.Y., Delaware Valley Press).

DEBO, ANGIE. 1940. *And Still the Waters Run* (Princeton, Princeton University Press).

DE COU, GEORGE. 1932. "The Indian Reservation at Indian Mills." *Mt. Holly Herald*, 15 April, 1932.

DEEDS, as bound in the Archives and History Bureau, New Jersey State Library, Trenton.

DELORIA, VINE, JR. 1967. *Custer Died for Your Sins, An Indian Manifesto* (New York, MacMillan).

—— 1973. *God is Red* (New York, Grosset & Dunlap).

DICKSON, CHARLES. 1886. "Agent's Report, Fort Simcoe, Washington Territory." In: *U. S. House of Representatives, Executive Documents. 2nd Session, 49th Congress, Department of the Interior* (Washington, D.C., U.S. Government Printing Office).

DOWNES, RANDOLPH. 1940. *Council Fires on the Upper Ohio, A Narrative of Indian Affairs in the Upper Ohio Valley until 1795* (Pittsburgh, University of Pittsburgh Press).

—— 1945. "A Crusade for Indian Reform, 1922–1934." *Miss. Valley Hist. Rev.* 32, 3: pp. 331–354.

DRUCKER, PHILIP. 1958. *The Native American Brotherhoods: Modern Inter-Tribal Organization on the Northwest Coast.* Bureau of American Ethnology *Bulletin* 168 (Washington D.C., U.S. Government Printing Office).

EDWARDS, JONATHAN. 1822. *Memoirs of the Rev. David Brainerd; Missionary to the Indians on the Borders of New York, New Jersey, and Pennsylvania: Chiefly taken from his own Diary . . .[added to] by S. E. Dwight* (New Haven, S. Converse; first printed 1749).

EKLAND, ROY E. 1969. "The 'Indian Problem,' Pacific Northwest, 1879." *Oregon Hist. Quart.* 70, 2: pp. 101–137.

ELKIN, A. P. 1951. "Reaction and Interaction: A Food Gathering People and European Settlement in Australia." *Amer. Anthropologist* 53: pp. 164–186.

FENTON, WILLIAM N. 1955. "Factionalism in American Indian Society." *International Congress of Anthropological & Ethnological Science, 4th, Vienna, 1952* 2: pp. 330–340.

—— 1971. "The Iroquois in History." In: Eleanor Burke Leacock and Nancy Oestreich Lurie, editors, *North American Indians in Historical Perspective* (New York, Random House), pp. 129–168.

FIRTH, RAYMOND W. 1929. *Primitive Economics of the New Zealand Maori* (New York, E. P. Dutton & Co).

FISHER, EDGAR JACOB. 1911. *New Jersey as a Royal Province, 1738 to 1776* (New York, Columbia University Press).

FOREMAN, GRANT. 1932. *Indian Removal: The Emigration of the Five Civilized Tribes* (Norman, University of Oklahoma Press).

—— 1946. *The Last Trek of the Indians* (Chicago, University of Chicago Press).

FRENCH, DAVID H. 1948. "Factionalism in Isleta Pueblo." *Monographs of the American Ethnological Society*, No. 14 (Seattle, University of Washington Press).

GARDINER, ABRAHAM S. 1888. *Tom Quick: or the Era of Frontier Settlement. Notes Suggested by the Legend of the Delaware by Hon. William Bross* (Chicago, Knight & Leonard Co.).

GEARING, FRED. 1962. *Priests & Warriors*. American Anthropological Association *Memoir* No. 93.

GIPSON, LAWRENCE HENRY. 1958–1969. *The British Empire before the American Revolution* (Caldwell, Idaho, the Caxton Press, and New York, Alfred A. Knopf).

HAAS, THEODORE H. 1957. "The Legel Aspects of Indians from 1887 to 1957." In: George E. Simpson and Milton J. Yinger, editors, *American Indians and American Life* [whole issue of] *Annals Acad. Polit. and Social Science* **311**.

HAGAN, WILLIAM T. 1956. "Private Property, The Indians' Door to Civilization." *Ethnohistory* **3**, 2: pp. 126–137.

HAGERTY, LEWIS M. 1960. "The Brainerds and Brotherton." *Bergen County Historical Society Papers* (*Revolutionary War Round Table Papers*), pp. 68–82.

HAINES, FRANCIS. 1950. "Problems of Indian Policy." *Pacific Northwest Quart.* **41**: pp. 206 ff.

HALLET, L. F. 1959. "The Colonial Invasion of Hereditary Lands." *Bull. Mass. Archaeol. Soc.* **20**: pp. 34–37.

HALLOWELL, A. I. 1945. "Sociopsychological Aspects of Acculturation." In: Ralph Linton, editor, *The Science of Man in World Crisis* (New York, Columbia University Press), pp. 171–200.

—— 1946. "Some Psychological Characteristics of Northeastern Indians." In Frederick Johnson, editor, *Man in Northeastern North America. Papers of the Robert S. Peabody Foundation for Archaeology* **3**: pp. 195–225.

—— 1957. "The Backwash of the Frontier: The Impact of the Indian on American Culture." In: Walker D. Wyman and Clifton B. Kroeber, editors, *The Frontier in Prespective* (Madison, University of Wisconsin Press), pp. 229–258.

HARPER, ALLEN G. 1947. "Canada's Indian Administration: The Treaty System." *America Indigena* **7**: pp. 129–148.

HARRISON, GORDON SCOTT. 1972. "The Alaska Native Claims Settlement Act 1971" *Arctic* **25**, 3: pp. 232–233.

HECKEWELDER, JOHN G. E. 1887. *An Account of the Indian Nations who once inhabited Pennsylvania and the Neighboring States*. In: *Trans. Hist. and Lit. Committee of the Amer. Philos. Soc.* **1** [1819, reprinted 1876, 1881].

HERTZBERG, HAZEL W. 1971. *The Search for an American Indian Identity: Modern Pan-Indian Movements* (Syracuse, Syracuse University Press).

HICKEY, NEIL. 1973. "Was the Truth Buried at Wounded Knee?" *T. V. Guide*, Dec. 1; 8; 15; 22, 1973.

HILL, GEORGE BIRBECK, editor 1904. *Boswell's Life of Johnson* (New York, Harper & Brothers).

HOFFMAN, BERNARD G. n.d. "Tribal Distribution in the Middle and Northern Appalachians [*ca.* 1600–1748]." MS. Report, 1961.

—— 1964. "Observations on Certain Ancient Tribes of the Northern Appalachian Province." *Bureau Amer. Ethnol. Bull.* **191**: pp. 191–246. (Anthropological Papers No. 70. Washington, D.C., U.S. Government Printing Office).

HOLM, THOMAS CAMPANIUS. 1834. *A Short Description of the Province of New Sweden, now called by the English Pennsylvania . . .* (translated by Peter S. Du Ponceau) (Philadelphia, Historical Society of Pennsylvania).

HUNT, GEORGE P. 1940. *The Wars of the Iroquois, A Study of Inter-Tribal Trade Relations* (Madison, University of Wisconsin Press).

HUNTER, WILLIAM A. 1954. "The Ohio, The Indians' Land." *Pennsylvania History* **21**, 4: pp. 338–350.

—— 1960. *Forts on the Pennsylvania Frontier, 1753–1758* (Harrisburg, Pennsylvania Historical and Museum Commission).

—— 1961. "The Walking Purchase." *Historic Pennsylvania Leaflet*, No. 24 (Harrisburg, Pennsylvania Historical and Museum Commission).

—— 1974 a. "Moses (Tunda) Tatamy, Delaware Indian Diplomat." In: *A Delaware Indian Symposium*, H. C. Kraft, editor, Pennsylvania Historical and Museum Commission, Anthropological Series, No. 4, Harrisburg.

—— 1974 b. "A Note on the Unalachtigo." In: *op. cit.*

HUNTINGTON. (The Henry E. Huntington Library and Art Gallery, San Marino, California. "LO" followed by a serial number refers to documents in the Lord Loudoun Collection.)

HUSTON, GERALDINE. 1950. *Oratam of the Hackensacks* (Paramus, N.J.).

JACKSON, HELEN HUNT. 1881. *A Century of Dishonor* (Boston, Harper and Brothers).

JACOBS, WILBUR R. 1950. *Diplomacy and Indian Gifts: Anglo-French Rivalry along the Ohio and Northwest Frontiers. 1748–1763* (Stanford, Stanford University Press).

JENNINGS, FRANCIS. 1974. "The Delaware Indians in the Covenant Chain." In: *A Delaware Indian Symposium*, H. C. Kraft, editor, Pennsylvania Historical and Museum Commission, Anthropological Series, No. 4, Harrisburg.

JOHNSON, AMANDUS. 1911. *Swedish Settlements on Delaware, 1638–1644* (New York, D. Appleton & Co.).

JORGENSON, JOSEPH. 1972. *The Sun Dance Religion: Power for the Powerless* (Chicago, University of Chicago Press).

JOSEPHY, ALVIN M., JR. 1965. *The Nez Percé Indians and the Opening of the Northwest* (New Haven and London, Yale University Press).

—— 1973. "Wounded Knee and All That—What the Indians Want." *New York Times Sunday Magazine*, 18 March, 1973.

KAPPLER, C. J., compiler and editor. 1904. *Indian Affairs: Laws and Treaties* (Washington D.C., U.S. Government Printing Office).

KARDAS, SUSAN. 1971. "The People Bought This and The Clatsop Became Rich." Bryn Mawr College Dissertation, Published by University Microfilms.

KELSEY, RAYNER WICKERSHAM. 1917. *The Friends and the Indians, 1655–1917* (Philadelphia, Association of the Executive Committee of the Friends on Indian Affairs).

KENNY, JAMES. 1913. "Journal of James Kenny, 1761–1763." *Pennsylvania Mag. History and Biography* **37**: pp. 1–47, 152–201.

KNOWLES, NATHANIEL. 1940. "The Torture of Captives by the Indians of Eastern North America." *Proc. Amer. Philos. Soc.* **82**: pp. 151–225.

KROEBER, A. L. 1947. *Cultural and Natural Areas of Native North America* (Berkeley, University of California Press; previous edition, 1939).

KROEBER, THEODORA. 1967. *Ishi in Two Worlds* (Berkeley, University of California Press).

LA FARGE, OLIVER. 1940. *As Long as the Grass Shall Grow* (New York).

—— 1957. "Termination of Federal Supervision: Disintegration and American Indians." In: G. E. Simpson and J. M. Yinger, editors, *American Indians and American Life.* [whole issue of] *Annals Amer. Acad. Polit. and Social Science* **311**: pp. 41–46.

LANG, GOTTFRIED O. 1961–1962. "Economic Development and Self-Determination: The Northern Ute Case." In: Deward E. Walker, Jr., editor, *The Emergent Native Americans* (Boston, Little, Brown and Co., 1972; originally published in *Human Organization* **20** (1961–1962)): pp. 164–171.

LARRABEE, EDWARD McM. n.d., a. "The Yakima Indian Treaty: 1855–1955." Thesis, Reed College, 1955.

—— n.d., b. "The Political Relationship Between Indians and Europeans in Colonial Pennsylvania." MS. paper, University of Washington, 1957.

—— 1970. "New Jersey and the Fortified Frontier of the 1750's." Columbia University Dissertation, published by University Microfilms.

—— 1977. "The 'Jonathan Hampton Map' and Governor Bernard." *New Jersey History* (forthcoming.)

LEACH, DOUGLAS EDWARD. 1966. *The Northern Colonial Frontier, 1607–1763* (New York, Holt Rinehart & Winston).

LEACOCK, ELEANOR BURKE, and NANCY OESTREICH LURIE, editors. 1971. *North American Indians in Historical Perspective* (New York, Random House).

LEE, RICHARD B., and IRVEN DE VORE, editors. 1968. *Man the Hunter* (Chicago, Aldine Publishing Co).

LEIBY, ADRIAN C. 1964. *The Early Dutch and Swedish Settlers of New Jersey* (Princeton, Van Nostrand).

LEVINE, STUART, and NANCY O. LURIE. 1968. *The American Indian Today* (Everett/Edwards).

LILLY, ELI, C. F. VOEGELIN, ERMINIE WHEELER VOEGELIN, JOE E. PIERCE, PAUL WEER, GLEN A. BLACK, and GEORG K. NEUMANN. 1954. *Walam Olum or Red Score, the Migration Legend of the Lenni Lenape or Delaware Indians* (Indianapolis, Indiana Historical Society).

LINTON, RALPH. 1940. *Acculturation in Seven American Tribes* (New York, D. Appleton Century Co.).

LOWIE, R. H. 1920. *Primitive Society* (New York, Boni & Liveright).

LURIE, NANCY OESTREICH. 1957. "The Indian Claims Commission Act." In: G. E. Simpson and J. M. Yinger, editors, *American Indians and American Life* [whole issue of] *Annals Amer. Acad. Polit. and Social Science* **311**: pp. 65–70.

—— 1958. "Indian Cultural Adjustment to European Civilization." In: James Morton Smith, editor, *Seventeenth Century America*, pp. 33–60 (Chapel Hill, The University of North Carolina Press).

MACLEOD, WILLIAM CHRISTIE. 1922. "The Family Hunting Territory and Lenape Political Organization." *Amer. Anthropologist* **24**: pp. 448–463.

—— 1928. *The American Indian Frontier* (New York, Alfred A. Knopf).

MCMAHON, REGINALD. 1971. "The Achter Col Colony on the Hackensack." *New Jersey History* **89**: pp. 221–240.

MCNICKLE, D'ARCY. 1957. "Indian and European: Indian-White Relations from Discovery to 1887." In: G. E. Simpson and J. M. Yinger, editors, *American Indians and American Life* [whole issue of] *Annals Acad. Polit. and Social Science* **311**: pp. 1–11.

—— 1971. *Indian Man: A Life of Oliver La Farge* (Bloomington, Indiana University Press).

—— 1973. *Native American Tribalism: Indian Survivals and Renewals* (New York, Oxford University Press).

MCWHORTER, LUCULLUS VIRGIL. 1952. *Hear Me, My Chiefs* (Caldwell, Idaho, Caxon Printers, Ltd.).

MALINOWSKI, BRONISLAW. 1945. *The Dynamics of Culture Change* (New Haven, Yale University Press).

MANYPENNY, GEORGE W. 1854. "Report of the Commissioner of Indian Affairs." *U.S. Senate Executive Documents, 33rd Congress, 1854–'55, the Report of the Secretary of the Interior*, pp. 218 ff.

—— 1855. "Report of the Commissioner of Indian Affairs." *U.S. Senate Executive Documents, 1st Session, 34th Congress, 1855–'56, The Report of the Secretary of the Interior*, pp. 332 ff.

—— 1880. *Our Indian Wards* (Cincinnati, Robert Clarke & Co.).

MARRIOTT, ALICE. 1948. *Maria: The Potter of San Ildefenso* (Norman, University of Oklahoma Press).

MEKEEL, SCUDDER. 1943. "A Short History of the Teton Dakota." *North Dakota Hist. Quart.* **10**: pp. 136–205.

MERCER, HENRY C. 1924. "The Origin of Log Houses in the United States." *Papers Read Before the Bucks County Historical Society* **5**: pp. 568–583.

MERRIAM, LEWIS, and associates. 1928. *The Problem of Indian Administration* (Baltimore, Institute for Government Research).

MIDDLETON, JOSEPH S. 1932. "Early Days in Crosswicks." *Mount Holly Herald*, 7 Oct., 1932.

MOONEY, JAMES. 1911. "The Passing of the Delaware Nation." *Proc. Miss. Valley Hist. Assoc.* **3**: pp. 329–340.

—— 1965. *The Ghost Dance Religion and the Sioux Outbreak of 1890* (edited and abridged, with an introduction by Anthony F. C. Wallace) (Chicago, University of Chicago Press, original publication 1896).

NEILL, EDWARD D. 1876. *The Founders of Maryland as Portrayed in Manuscripts, Provincial Records, and Early Documents* (Albany, N.Y., Joel Munsell, Printer).

NELSON, WILLIAM W. 1883, 1885. "Biographic Notes" (as editor of *N.J. Archives*).

NEVILL, SAMUEL. 1761. *The Acts of the General Assembly of the Province of New Jersey from . . . 1753 to . . . 1761* (Woodbridge, New Jersey, James Parker).

NEWCOMB, WILLIAM W., JR. 1956. *The Culture and Acculturation of the Delaware Indians*. Anthropological Papers, Museum of Anthropology, University of Michigan, No. 10.

N.J. Archives. 1880–1931. [Binders' title for] William A. Whitehead, William Nelson, & F. W. Ricord, editors, *Documents Relating to the Colonial History of the State of New Jersey* (Newark, Patterson, and Trenton, N.J.).

N.J. Assembly Journal. MS. bound as "A Journal of the Proceedings of the General Assembly of New Jersey [for the Colonial period]" the Archives and History Bureau, New Jersey State Library, Trenton.

N.J. Assembly Votes. MS. bound as "Votes of the New Jersey Assembly." A continuation into the nineteenth century of the N.J. Assembly Journal, in the Archives and History Bureau, New Jersey State Library, Trenton.

NEW JERSEY BELL. 1974. "First Reservation." In: *Tel-News*. October, 1974.

N.Y. Colonial Documents. 1853–1887. [Binders' title for] O'Callaghan, Edmund Bailey, & Berthold Fernow, editors, *Documents Relative to the Colonial History of New York* (Albany, N.Y., Weed & Parsons, Co., Printers).

OLNEY, BEN. Personal communications with the author, 1957–1958.

OPLER, MORRIS E. 1945. "Themes as Dynamic Forces in Culture." *Amer. Jour. Sociology* **51**: pp. 198–206.

—— 1946. "An Application of the Theory of Themes in Culture." *Jour. Washington Acad. of Sciences* **36**, 5: pp. 137–166.

—— 1949. "The Context of Themes." *Amer. Anthropologist.* **51**: pp. 323–325.

—— 1959. "Component, Assemblage, and Theme in Cultural Integration and Differentiation." *Amer. Anthropologist.* **61**: pp. 955–964.

—— 1968. "The Themal Approach in Current Anthropology and its Application to North Indian Data." *Southwestern Jour. Anthropology* **24**, 3: pp. 215–227.

OSWALT, WENDELL H. 1973. *This Land Was Theirs: A Study of the North American Indian* (Second Edition, New York, John Wiley & Sons).

PARGELLIS, STANLEY M. 1936. "Braddock's Defeat." *Amer. Hist. Rev.* **61**: pp. 253–268.

PEARCE, ROY HARVEY. 1953. *The Savages of America, A Study of the Indian and the Idea of Civilization* (Baltimore, Johns Hopkins Press).

—— 1957. "The Metaphysics of Indian Hating." *Ethnohistory* **4**, 1: pp. 27–40.
Pennsylvania Colonial Records. 1838–1853. [Binders' title for] *The Minutes of the Provincial Council of Pennsylvania . . .* [1683–1775] (Philadelphia and Harrisburg).
PETERSON, HELEN L. 1957. "American Indian Political Participation." In: G. E. Simson and J. M. Yinger, editors, *American Indians and American Life* [whole issue of] *Annals Amer. Acad. of Polit. and Social Science* **311**: pp. 116–126.
PHILIP, KENNETH. 1973. "John Collier and the Crusade to Protect Indian Religious Freedom, 1920–1926." *Jour. Ethnic Studies* **1**, 1: pp. 22–38.
POMFRET, JOHN EDWIN. 1964. *The New Jersey Proprietors and Their Lands, 1664–1776* (Princeton, D. Van Nostrand Co.).
PRUCHA, FRANCIS P. 1962. *American Indian Policy in the Formative Years: The Indian Trade and Intercourse Acts, 1790–1834* (Cambridge, Harvard University Press).
QUINLAN, JAMES ELDRIDGE. 1851. *Tom Quick the Indian Slayer and the Pioneers of Minisink and Wawarsink* (Monticello, N.Y.).
RELANDER, CLICK. 1956. *Drummers and Dreamers* (Caldwell, Idaho, Caxton Printers, Ltd.).
RUBY, ROBERT H., and JOHN A. BROWN. 1965. *Half-Sun on the Columbia (a Biography of Chief Moses)* (Norman, University of Oklahoma Press).
RUTTENBERG, EDWARD MANNING. 1872. *History of the Indian Tribes on Hudson's River* (Albany, N.Y., Joel Munsell, N.Y.).
SCHLESIER, KARL H. 1974. "Action Anthropology and the Southern Cheyenne." ("American Indian Action: 1") *Current Anthropology* **15**, 3: pp. 277–283, 289–299, 302–303.
SCHMECKEBIER, L. F. 1927. *The Office of Indian Affairs, its History, Activities and Organization* (Baltimore, Johns Hopkins Press).
SERVICE, ELMAN R. 1954. *Spanish-Guarani Relations in Early Colonial Paraguay.* Anthropological Papers, Museum of Anthropology, University of Michigan, No. 9.
—— 1955. "Indian-European Relations in Colonial Latin America." *Amer. Anthropologist* **57**: pp. 411–425.
—— 1971. *Profiles in Ethnology* (Revised edition [originally published as *A Profile of Primitive Culture*] New York, Harper & Row).
SESSION LAWS. 1741–1756. [Abbreviation for] *The Session Laws of the Province of New Jersey* (printed at the close of each session, and bound for the above dates in the Archives and History Bureau, New Jersey State Library, Trenton).
SHANKEL, GEORGE EDGAR. 1945. "The Development of Indian Policy in British Columbia." Seattle, University of Washington Dissertation.
SHARP, LAURISTON. 1952. "Steel Axes for Stone-Age Australians." *Human Organization* **11**, 1:
SHURTLEFF, HAROLD E. 1939. *The Log Cabin Myth, A Study of Early Dwellings of the English Colonists in North America* (Edited with introduction by Samuel Eliot Morison) (Cambridge, Harvard University Press).
SHY, JOHN. 1965. *Toward Lexington, the Role of the British Army in the Coming of the American Revolution* (Princeton, Princeton University Press).
SMITH, HENRY NASH. 1950. *Virgin Land, The American West as Symbol and Myth* (Cambridge, Harvard University Press).
SMITH, SAMUEL. 1765. *The History of the Colony of Nova-Caesaria, or New Jersey . . .* (Burlington, N.J., James Parker).
SPECK, FRANK G. 1915. "The Family Hunting Band as the Basis of Algonkian Social Organization." *Amer. Anthropologist* **17**: pp. 289–305.
SPICER, EDWARD H., editor. 1961. *Perspectives in American Indian Culture Change* (Chicago, University of Chicago Press).
—— 1962. *Cycles of Conquest* (Tucson, University of Arizona Press).
—— 1971. "Presistent Cultural Systems." *Science* **174**, 4011: pp. 795–800.
SPINDLER, GEORGE D. and LOUISE S. 1957. "American Indian Personality Types and their Socio-Cultural Roots." In: G. E. Simpson and J. M. Yinger, editors *American Indians and American Life* [whole issue of] *Annals Amer. Acad. Polit. and Social Science* **311**: pp. 147–157.
STEINER, STAN. 1968. *The New Indians* (New York, Harper and Row).
STERN, THEODORE. 1961. "Livelihood and Tribal Organization on the Klamath Reservation." *Human Organization* **20**: pp. 172–180.
STEVENS, ISAAC I. 1854. "Superintendent's Report, Washington Territory, 1854." In: *U.S. Senate Executive Documents, 33rd Congress, 1854–'55, the Report of the Secretary of the Interior,* pp. 455–456.
STEWARD, JULIAN. 1955. *Theory of Culture Change: The Methodology of Multilinear Evolution* (Urbana, University of Illinois Press).
SURVEYORS GENERAL OFFICE. Basse Book. MS. in Archives and History Bureau, New Jersey State Library, Trenton.
TANNER, EDWIN P. 1908. *The Province of New Jersey, 1664–1738* (New York, Columbia University Press).
TAYLOR, GEORGE ROGERS, editor. 1956. *The Turner Thesis Concerning the Role of the Frontier in American History* (Revised edition, Boston, D.C. Heath & Co.).
TAYLOR, SAMUEL. 1927. "The Origins of the Dawes Act of 1887." Harvard University Thesis, Philip Washburn Prize.
THAYER, THEODORE. 1943. *Israel Pemberton, King of the Quakers* (Philadelphia, Historical Society of Pennsylvania).
THURMAN, MELBURNE D. 1974. "Delaware Social Organization." In: *A Delaware Indian Symposium,* H. C. Kraft, editor, Pennsylvania Historical and Museum Commission, Anthropological Series, No. 4, Harrisburg.
THWAITES, REUBEN GOLD, editor. 1904–1907. *Early Western Travels* (Cleveland).
TRELEASE, ALLEN W. 1960. *Indian Affairs in Colonial New York: The Seventeenth Century* (Ithaca, N.Y., Cornell University Press).
—— 1962. "The Iroquois and the Western Fur Trade: A Problem in Interpretation." *Miss. Valley Hist. Rev.* **69**: pp. 32–51.
The Trenton Federalist (Trenton, N.J.).
UHLER, SHERMAN P. 1951. *Pennsylvania's Indian Relations to 1754* (Allentown, Pa.).
UNITED STATES BOARD OF INDIAN COMMISSIONERS. n.d. *Annual Reports* to the Secretary of the Interior, 1869.
UTLEY, ROBERT M. 1953. "The Celebrated Peace Policy of General Grant." *North Dakota History* **20**, 3: pp. 121–142.
VAUGHAN, ALDEN T. 1965. *New England Frontier: Puritans and Indians, 1620–1675* (Boston, Little, Brown & Co).
VAN EVERY, DALE. 1966. *Disinherited: The Lost Birthright of the American Indian* (New York, Avon Library Books).
VOLWEILER, ALBERT TANGEMEN. 1926. *George Croghan and the Westward Movement, 1741–1782* (Cleveland, Arthur H. Clark Co.).
WADELL, JACK O., and O. MICHAEL WATSON, editors. 1971. *The American Indian in Urban Society* (Boston, Little, Brown & Co.).

WALKER, DEWARD E., JR., editor. 1972. *The Emergent Native Americans* (Boston, Little, Brown and Co.).

WALLACE, A. F. C. 1947. "Women, Land & Society: Three Aspects of Aboriginal Delaware Life (Section II, The Status of the Delaware Indians in the Iroquois Confederacy)." *Pennsylvania Archaeologist* **17**, 1-4.

—— 1949. *King of the Delawares: Teedyuscung, 1700-1763* (Philadelphia, University of Pennsylvania Press).

—— 1951. "Some Psychological Determinants of Culture Change in an Iroquoian Community." In: William N. Fenton, editor, *Symposium on Local Diversity in Iroquois Culture. Bureau Amer. Ethnol. Bull.* **149**: pp. 55-76.

—— 1952. "The Modal Personality Structure of the Tuscarora Indians." *Bureau Amer. Ethnol. Bull.* **150**.

—— 1956. "New Religions among the Delaware Indians, 1600-1900." *Southwestern Jour. Anthropology* **12**: pp. 1-21.

—— 1969. *The Death & Rebirth of the Seneca* (New York, Random House).

WALLACE, PAUL A. W. 1945. *Conrad Weiser, 1696-1760, Friend of Colonist and Mohawk* (Philadelphia, University of Pennsylvania Press).

—— 1961. *Indians in Pennsylvania* (Harrisburg, Pennsylvania Historical and Museum Commission).

WASHBURN, WILCOMB E. 1957. *The Governor and the Rebel: A History of Bacon's Rebellion in Virginia* (Chapel Hill, University of North Carolina Press).

WATKINS, ARTHUR V. 1957. "Termination of Federal Supervision: The Removal of Restrictions over Indian Property and Person." In: G. E. Simpson and J. M. Yinger, editors, *American Indians and American Life* [whole issue of] *Annals Amer. Acad. Polit. and Social Science* **311**: pp. 47-55.

WEBB, WALTER PRESCOTT. 1952. *The Great Frontier* (Boston, Houghton Mifflin Co.).

WESLAGER, C. A. 1943. *Delaware's Forgotten Folk, the Story of the Moors and Nanticokes*.

—— 1944. "The Delaware Indians as Women." *Jour. Washington Acad. of Sciences* **34**: pp. 381-388.

—— 1972. *The Delaware Indians: A History* (New Brunswick, Rutgers University Press).

WHITE, ROBERT A. 1974. "Value Themes of the Native American Tribalistic Movement among the South Dakota Sioux. ("American Indian Action: 2") *Current Anthropology* **15**, 3: pp. 284-289.

WILSON, EDMUND. 1960. *Apologies to the Iroquois* (New York, Random House).

WITTFOGEL, KARL AUGUST. 1959. "The Theory of Oriental Society." In: Morton H. Fried, editor, *Readings in Anthropology* **2**: pp. 179-198. (Second edition, New York, Thomas Y. Crowell Co.).

WOOD, C. E. S. 1969. "Private Journal, 1879." *Oregon Hist. Quart.* **70**, 2: pp. 139-170.

WOODWARD, MAJOR E. M., and JOHN F. HAGEMAN. 1883. *A History of Burlington and Mercer Counties* (Philadelphia, Everts & Peck).

YAPLE. ROBERT L. 1968. "Braddock's Defeat: The Theories and a Reconsideration." *Jour. Soc. Army Hist. Research* **46**, 188: pp. 194-201.

ZEISBERGER, DAVID. 1910. *History of Northern American Indians* (Reprinted in *the Ohio Archaeol. and Hist. Quart.* **19**, 1 & 2).

ZIMMERMAN, ALBRIGHT G. 1974. "European Trade Relations in the 17th and 18th Centuries." In: *A Delaware Indian Symposium*, H. C. Kraft, editor, Pennsylvania Historical and Museum Commission, Anthropological Series, No. 4, Harrisburg.

ZIMMERMAN, WILLIAM, JR. 1957. "The Role of the Bureau of Indian Affairs since 1933." In: G. E. Simpson and J. M. Yinger, editors, *American Indians and American Life*. [whole issue of] *Annals Amer. Acad. Polit. and Social Science* **311**: pp. 31-30.

INDEX

Aberle, David P., 37
Acculturation, 7
Acrelius, Israel, 4
Africa, 33
Agricultural, agriculture, 5, 29
Alaska, 34
Alaska Native Claims Settlement Act, 41
Albany, 4
Alcatraz, 36
Algonquian, 3
Allinson, Samuel, 8, 9, 10, 13
Allinson, Samuel (2nd), 3, 5, 9, 10, 11, 13, 15, 16, 17, 18, 29
Allinson, W. J., 5, 17
American Revolution, 23, 25
Ancocus Indians (Delaware), 8
Anglo-American, *passim*
Apache (Indians), 35, 36
Assembly, Legislative, of New Jersey, 4–5, 7, 8, 9, 10, 13, 14, 15, 16, 17, 23, 24, 29
Assimilation, 38
Australia(n), 30, 33

Bacon, Nathaniel (Virginia Rebellion leader), 27
Bain, John (N. J. petitioner), 5, 15
Barber, John W., 5, 13, 17, 24
Barth, Fredrik, 37
Beans, see Crops and foods
Belcher, Jonathan (governor of N. J.), 4, 7
Berkhofer, Robert F., Jr., 28
Bernard, Francis (later Sir, governor of N. J.), 9, 10, 11, 12, 13, 14, 15, 19, 24, 29, 30
Berries, see Crops and foods
Bethel (community or band of Lenape), see Cranbury
Bevier, Abraham Garret, 21, 42
Billington, Ray Allen, 43
Bisbee, Henry H., 3, 17
Blacks, Black people, 8, 22
Bloomfield, Joseph (Governor of N. J.), 17
Board of Indian Commissioners, United States, 28, 29
Boone, Daniel (American frontiersman), 41
Boone, Thomas (governor of N. J.), 13
Boquet, Henry, Colonel, 7
Boyce, George A., 36
Braddock, Edward, General, 7, 23
Brainerd, David (missionary), 5, 27
Brainerd, John (missionary, brother of David), 5, 7, 8, 9, 11, 13, 14, 15, 20, 24, 27
Brainerd, Thomas, 5
British Columbia, 28
Bross, William, 21, 42
Brotherton (community or band of Lenape), 3, 5, 7, 9, 11, 12, 13, 14, 15, 16, 17, 18, 19, 20, 21, 22, 23, 24, 25, 26, 27, 28, 29, 30, 38
Brown, Dee, 27, 36
Brunner, Edward M., 39
Bumpo, Natty (fictional frontiersman in James Fenimore Cooper books), 42
Burlington, 5, 9, 11

Bureau of Indian Affairs, United States Department of the Interior, 28, 36
Bureau of Reclamation, United States Department of the Interior, 30
Bushy Run, Battle of, 7

California, 27, 34
Calvin, Batholemew (Delaware schoolmaster, son of Stephen Calvin), 13, 14, 17, 24
Calvin, Stephen (Delaware interpreter and schoolmaster), 9, 11, 13
Canada, Canadian, 7, 28, 34, 43
Canasetego (Onondaga Chief), 23
Captives, 19
Casteneda, Carlos, 36
Cattle, see Livestock
Cayuga (Iroquois Indians), 11
Chagnon, Napoleon A., 18
Chain, "Great Chain of Friendship," 19
Charter, Royal English, for N. J., 4, 10
Cherokee (Indians), 18, 39
Cherokee Nation v. *State of Georgia*, 21
Cheyenne (Indians), 36
Children, Indian, 8
Chippewas (Chippewa Indians), 18
Christian, Christianity, 21, 26, 28
Civil War, United States, 38
Codere, Helen, 39, 42
College of New Jersey, see Princeton
Collier, John (commissioner of Indian Affairs) 27, 29, 35, 36, 37, 43
Colonial, Colonists, see "Anglo-American"
Columbia (River) Plateau, 28
Colville Reservation (Washington State), 29
Common Measure, or Common Factor (see also Malinowski), 19
Conflict, foci of, among themes, 22, 23, 24, 25, 26
Contract, "sancity of," 20, 26
Corn, see Crops and foods
Corps of Engineers, U. S. Army, 30
Costo, Rupert, 28
Court of Indian Claims, 30
Crafts, 36
Cranbury (community and band of Lenape, called "Bethel Indians"), 5, 7, 8, 9, 10, 11, 13, 15, 17, 19, 22, 24, 27
Creatures (i.e., Anglo-American cattle), see Livestock
Crisis, of intercultural relationship, 32, 34, 35
Croghan, George (deputy agent, Indian Affairs), 11
Crops and foods, native American, 3, 4, 14, 18, 19, 20, 30
Crosswicks (community and band of Lenape), 5, 7, 8, 9, 11, 13, 15, 19, 22, 23
Crumb, Fred W., 21, 42

Dakota (Indians), 35
Dakota (region and events in), 27

Dawes Act (see also Indian Allotment Act of 1887, General Allotment Act), 29, 35, 43
Debo, Angie, 27, 28
De Cou, George, 3, 13, 15, 17
Deeds (in N. J. Archives), 8, 9, 10, 11, 12, 13, 18
Deerfield, 14
Delaware (Indians), Delawares; Ancocus; Mauhkennuks; Munsi; Opings; Pompton; Sand Hill; Unami, 3, 4, 5, 7, 8, 9, 10, 11, 12, 13, 14, 15, 16, 17, 18, 19, 20, 21, 22, 23, 24, 25, 26, 28, 29, 30, 38
Deloria, Vine, 36
Development of land, in Anglo-American terms, see Resources
Dickson, Charles, 28
Directed culture contact, 32, 34, 37, 41, 42, 43
Disease, 4, 41, 42
Downes, Randolph, 7, 35
Dozier, Edward P., 39
Dreams, dream interpretation, 19
Drucker, Philip, 36
Duquesne, Fort, 7
Dutch, 4, 19

Eastern woodlands, culture area, 19, 23
Easton, Pa., conference at, 9, 10, 11, 13, 18, 20, 28
Edge Pillock, see Brotherton
Edwards, Jonathan, 5
Egohohowen (Minisink Indian leader), 10, 11
Ekland, Roy E., 28
Elkin, A. P., 27, 30, 33
Erie (Indians), 4
Euro-American, see Anglo-American
European, 19, 27

Fallen Timbers, Battle of, 35
Farmer, farming, food production (Anglo-American; see also Agriculture), 20, 22, 23, 24, 25, 26, 29, 30, 40, 41, 42–43
Fenton, William N., 22, 29
Firth, Raymond W., 27, 30, 32
Fisher, Edgar Jacob, 4
Five (or Six) Nations, see Iroquois
Flathead (Indians), 34
Food (native North American), see Crops and food
Foreman, Grant, 18, 28
France, French, 7, 19, 23
Franklin, William (governor of N. J.), 14, 15
Franklin County, Kansas, 18
French, David H., 39, 42
Freylinghuysen, F. T. (U. S. senator from N. J.), 18
Friends, Society of, see Quakers
Frontier (attacks, defenses, forts, militia, posts, raids on), 7, 9, 10, 23, 42–43
Fur, fur-bearing animals, fur trade, 4, 22, 27

49

Game, see Hunting
Gantowisas (ceremonial Iroquoian term), 22
Gardiner, Abraham S., 21, 42
Gearing, Fred, 39
General Allotment Act, see Dawes Act
Generosity, 19, 26, 40
Ghandi, 36
Gipson, Lawrence Henry, 25
Grant, Ulysses S. (U. S. president), 28
Great Awakening, 5, 24
Greenville, Treaty of, 35
Guardian, see Superintendent

Haas, Theodore H., 29
Hagan, William T., 29
Hagerty, Lewis M., 9
Haida (Indians), 34
Haines, Francis, 33
Hallet, L. F., 27
Hallowell, A. I., 18, 19, 41
Hardy, Josiah (governor of N. J.), 13
Harper, Allen G., 28
Harrison, Gordon Scott, 41
Heckewelder, John G. E., 4
Herding, 20
Hickey, Neil, 28
Hill, George Birbeck, 21
Hithquoquean (Delaware spokesman), 22
Hoffman, Bernard G., 4, 22, 23
Hogs, see Livestock
Holm, Thomas Campanius, 22
Honor, 19, 22
Hopi (Indians), 41
Housatonic (Indians), 18
Hudson River and Valley, 5, 19, 22
Hudson's Bay Company, 27
Hunt, George P., 4, 22
Hunt, John (Quaker preacher), 15
Hunter(s), Hunting (see also Game), 4, 5, 8, 9, 10, 11, 12, 17, 18, 19, 22, 23, 24, 27, 30, 40
Hunter, William A., 4, 5, 7, 9, 22, 23
Huntington Library, 8
Huron (Indians), 4
Huston, Geraldine, 4
Hydraulic Society, 30

Indian(s), *passim*; and see categories: Delaware; Indian Individuals; and Iroquois; and following entries: Algonquain; Apache; Cherokee; Cheyenne; Chippewas; Dakota; Erie; Flathead; Haida; Hopi; Housatonic; Huron; Klamath; Kwakiutl; Mandan; Menominee; Mohican; Navajo; Nez Percé; Nootka; Pueblos; Shawnee; Shoshone; Stockbridge; Susquehanna; Utes; Wishram; Yahi; Yakima; Yaqui
Indian Allotment Act, see Dawes Act
Indian individuals (leaders, spokesmen, interpreters, schoolmasters), see: Calvin, Bartholemew; Calvin, Stephen; Canasetego; Egohohowen; Hithquoquean; Jacobs, Captain; Joseph, Chief; King, Thomas; Newcastle; Pompshire, John; Scollitchy; Shingas; Teedyuscung; Tagashata; Tattamy, Moses; Tohahoyo
Indian haters and Indian lovers, 43
Indian Mills, see Brotherton
Indian Reorganization Act, 36, 43

Indian towns, 3, 5, 12, 13
Intercessor, see Superintendent
Iroquoian language, speakers, 19, 22
Iroquois (see also Five, or Six Nations, United Nations), 4, 10, 11, 19, 22, 23, 26, 38, 43 (and see Cayuga; Mingo; Mohawk; Oneida; Onondaga; Seneca)

Jackson, Helen Hunt, 22, 27
Jacobs, Captain (Delaware Indian leader), 22
Jacobs, Wilbur R., 25
Jennings, Francis, 4, 19, 23
Jesuit, 38
Johnson, Amandus, 4
Johnson, Samuel, Dr., 21
Johnson, William, Sir (Northern Colonies agent, Indian Affairs), 11, 23
Jorgenson, Joseph, 24, 28, 37, 41, 42
Joseph, Chief (Nez Percé Leader), 33
Josephy, Alvin M., 28, 33

Kansas, 18
Kappler, C. J., 28
Kardas, Susan, 27, 40
Kelsey, Rayner Wickersham, 28
Kenny, James, 23
Kin, see Residence
King, Thomas (Oneida chief), 10, 11
Klamath (Indians), 29, 43
Knowles, Nathaniel, 19
Kroeber, A. L., 4, 19
Kroeber, Theodora, 27
Kwakiutl (Indians), 30, 39

La Farge, Oliver, 27, 29, 36, 37, 43
Lake Michigan, 17
Land, claims and titles, 5, 9, 10, 27, 28, 29, 30
Land, sale of, by Indians to Anglo-Americans, 4, 8, 9, 10–11, 16–17, 27, 28, 29, 34, 41
Lang, Gottfried O., 30
Laramie, Fort, 27
Larrabee, Edward McM., 4, 7, 9, 21, 28, 30, 35
Leach, Douglas Edward, 3
Leacock, Eleanor Burke, 27, 29, 30, 36
Lease(s), leasing, 15, 23, 29
Lee, Richard B., 18
Leiby, Adrian C., 4
Lenape, or Lenni Lenape, see Delaware Indians
Lilly, Eli, 19, 22
Linton, Ralph, 32
Liquor, 8, 13, 14
Livestock (Anglo-American), 5, 10, 14, 20, 27, 36
Log buildings, 13
Lords of Trade, 4, 7, 11
Lotteries, 9, 21, 28
Lowie, R. H., 4
Lurie, Nancy Oestreich, 30; see also Leacock

MacLeod, William Christie, 4, 27
McMahon, Reginald, 4
McNickle, D'Arcy, 25, 27, 28, 29, 30, 37, 43
McWhorter, Lucullus Virgil, 30, 43
Maize, see Crops and food

Males, adult, see Men, Anglo-American; Men, Indian
Malinowski, Bronislaw, 19, 27, 33
Mandan (Indians), 30, 39
Manypenny, George, 27, 33
Marriott, Alice, 36
Marshall, John (U. S. chief justice), 21
Maryland, 7
Massachusetts, 3, 18
Matrilineal, see Residence
Matthews, Thomas (Virginia planter), 27
Mauhkennuks (Delawaran speaking Indians at New Stockbridge, N. Y.), 16
Maukesons, or Indian shoes (moccasins), 7
Mekeel, Scudder, 27, 30, 32
Mercer, Henry C., 13
Men, Anglo-American, 20, 25, 26, 40, 41
Men, Indian, 4, 5, 7, 8, 10, 15, 18, 19, 22, 23, 25, 26, 29, 40
Menominee (Indians), 17, 29, 43
Merriam, Lewis, 27, 28, 35
Mexican, Mexico, 38, 39
Middleton, Joseph S., 5
Mills (grain, grist, saw), 11, 12, 13, 14, 15, 16, 17, 20, 28
Millstone (river), 5
Mingo (Iroquois Indians on the Ohio), 7
Minisink Country, or Minisinks, 7, 9, 21, 23; see also Munsi, Minisink Indians
Minister, see Missions, Superintendent
Missions, Missionaries, 5, 13, 27, 28
Mohawk (Iroquois Indians), 10
Mohican (Indians), 4, 18
Montour, Henry (interpreter), 11
Mooney, James, 4, 42
Moore, Benjamin (N. J. landowner), 9
Morris, Robert Hunter (N. J. landowner, justice, Council member), 5
Mount Holly, 14
Mountain Men, 42
Movies, 36
Munsi (Delaware speaking) (see also Minisink Indians), 5, 9, 10, 18
Murder(s), 6, 21

Nails, 14, 23
Native American Brotherhood, 36
Native American Church, 38
Native North Americans, see Indians
Navajo (Indians), 30, 35, 36, 38, 43
Neill, Edward D., 22
Nelson, William W., 5, 7, 8, 9, 10
Nevill, Samuel, 8, 9, 10
Newark, 5
Newcastle (Iroquois chief), 23
Newcomb, William W., Jr., 3, 4, 5, 18, 19, 22, 23, 38
New Jersey, 3, 4, 5, 7, 8, 9, 10, 11, 12, 13, 14, 15, 17, 18, 19, 20, 21, 22, 23, 24, 26, 27, 28, 29, 30, 32, 38
N. J. Archives, 4, 5, 7, 8, 9, 10, 11, 12, 13, 14, 15, 19, 29, 30
N. J. Assembly Journal, 4, 9, 14, 15
N. J. Assembly Votes, 17
New Jersey Bell, 3
New Stockbridge, N. Y. (also Stockbridge Indians), 16, 17, 18
New York, 4, 8, 9, 13, 14, 16, 24, 27, 38, 43
N. Y. Colonial Documents, 19
Nez Percé (Indians), 29, 33

INDEX

Non-Directed culture contact, see Directed
Nootka (Indians), 34

Oklahoma, 38
Olney, Ben, 36
Oneida (Iroquois Indians), 10, 18
Onondaga (Iroquois Indian), 23
Opings (Delaware Indians), see Pompton Indians
Opler, Morris E., 18, 19
Oswalt, Wendel H., 30
Ownership of land, Delaware Indian concepts of, 4, 18–19, 25–26; Anglo-American concepts, see Real estate
Ownership, see Rights of Indians

Pacific Northwest, 27
Pargellis, Stanley M., 5
Patrilineal, see Residence
Paxton Boys, 21
Peace policy, 28
Pearce, Roy Harvey, 42
Pemberton, Israel (Pa. Assembly Member), 8
Penn, William, 9, 23
Pennsbury, 14, 23
Pennsylvania 4, 7, 8, 9, 10, 14, 19, 21, 22, 23, 24, 27, 37, 43
Pennsylvania Colonial Records, 11, 20, 22, 23
Peterson, Helen L., 29
Phases, Historical, 30, 32, 34, 35
Philip, Kenneth, 35, 37
Pomfret, John Edwin, 4
Pompshire, John (Delaware interpreter), 9
Pompton Indians (Delaware), 9, 10, 11
Pontiac's Rebellion or War, 14, 23
Population, Indian, 41–42
Presbyterians, 5, 6–7, 8, 13, 24, 28
Princeton (town, and college at), 13, 14, 24
Progressive Era, 36
Property, see Real estate
Proprietors (Boards of), 4, 10, 20, 23, 24
Protector, see Superintendent
Protestant-Ethic individualism, 37
Prucha, Francis P., 35
Pueblos, Rio Grande, 30, 38
Puyallup (river and reservation), 36

Quakers, 8, 9, 13, 15, 24, 28, 38
Quick, Tom (Indian slayer), 21, 42
Quinlan, James Eldridge, 21, 42

Raritan (river, and Lenape), 5, 8, 9
Real estate (also property), 20–21, 25, 26, 27, 29, 41
Registration (of friendly Delaware Indians), 7
Relander, Click, 30
Relocation policy, 30, 36
Removal policy, 30
Reservation, 3, 5, 21, 24, 26, 28, 29, 30
Residence, units, or pattern, native North American, 3, 4, 5, 18, 19, 22, 26, 40
Resource utilization (also development, underdevelopment), 20, 23–24, 29, 34, 40, 41
Revitalization, 38, 42
Rights of Indians (to hunt, fish, trap, gather, etc.), 9, 10, 11, 17–18, 28, 30

Rio Grande, 39
Roles (sexual), see Children; Men; Women
Ruby, Robert H., 29
Rum, see Liquor
Ruttenberg, Edward Manning, 4

Saint Lawrence, 39
Sand Hill Delaware (Indians), 18
Savages, 20, 40, 42
Scalp Bounty, 7–8
Schlesier, Karl H., 38
Schmeckebier, L. F., 27, 28, 35
Scollitchy (Delaware spokesman), 22
Seminole War, 27
Seneca (Iroquois Indians), 10
Senate, U. S., 28
Sequences, 3, 26–27, 30–39
Service, Elman R., 18, 27
Session Laws, 7, 8, 10
Shankel, George Edgar, 28
Sharp, Lauriston, 42
Shawano County, Wisc., 18
Shawnee (Indians), 7, 19, 35
Sheep, see Livestock
Shellfish, see Crops and foods
Shingas (Delaware Indian leader), 22
Shoshone (Indians), 34, 41
Shurtleff, Harold E., 13
Shy, John, 7, 25
Smallpox, 5
Smith, Henry Nash, 42
Smith, Edward P. (U. S. commissioner of Indian Affairs), 18
Smith (or Smyth), Frederick (Chief Justice of N. J.), 14
Smith, Samuel, 5, 8, 9, 10, 14, 15
Society in Scotland for Propagating Christian Knowledge, see Presbyterians
Southard, Samuel L. (N. J. legislator), 18
Southeast Asia, 36
Spain, Spanish, 28, 38
Speck, Frank G., 4
Spicer, Edward H., 18, 30, 32, 38, 39
Spicer, Jacob (N. J. Assembly member), 8, 9
Spindler, George D., 18, 19
Springer, Benjamin (N. J. landowner), 9, 11, 12
Stages, see Phases
Steiner, Stan, 36
Stern, Theodore, 29
Stevens, Isaac I. (governor of Washington Territory), 33
Steward, Julian, 18
Squash, see Crops and foods
Stanwix, Fort, 14
Stockbridge (Indians), see New Stockbridge
Sun Dance, 41
Superintendent, 13–14, 20, 24, 28
Surveyors General Office, 9
Susquehanna or Susquehannock (Indians), 4, 22, 27
Susquehanna River, 8, 22
Swedish, Swedes, 4, 13

Tagashata (Seneca chief), 10, 11
Tanner, Edwin P., 4
Tattamy, Moses (Delaware interpreter), 11
Taylor, George Rogers, 43

Taylor, Samuel, 29
Taxes (and tax free status, tax exemption), 9, 10, 21
Teedyuscung (Delaware Indian leader), 8, 9, 10, 20, 22, 23
Termination Policy, 29, 36, 38
Thayer, Theodore, 9, 23
Themes, Cultural, 18, 19, 20, 21, 22, 23, 24, 25, 26, 39–43
Thurman, Melburne D., 3, 4
Thwaites, Ruben Gold, 20, 23
Tohahoyo (Cayuga Indian leader), 11
Torture, see Captives
Traders, 7, 25, 27
Trail of Broken Treaties, 28
Trappers, 8, 42
Treaty (treaties, treaty conferences), 4, 7, 8, 9, 10–11, 15, 20, 21, 26, 28, 32, 33, 35, 37, 40
Trelease, Allen W., 4, 19
Trenton Federalist, 17
Tribes, 3, 26
Turner, Frederick Jackson, 42

Uhler, Sherman, P., 4
Unami (Delaware Indians), 5, 22, 23, 38
United Nations, see Iroquois
United States, 27, 36, 38
United States Board of Indian Commissioners, 29
Utes, Northern (Indians), 41
Uxorilocal, see Residence

Van Every, Dale, 36
Vanishing Indian theme, 24, 26, 39, 42
Vaughan, Alden T., 3, 27
Villages, see Residence
Vincentown, see Weepink
Virginia, 7, 27
Volweiler, Albert Tangeman, 11

Waddell, Jack O., 28, 37, 41
Walker, Deward E., 30
Walking Purchase, 9, 23
Wallace, A. F. C., 4, 8, 9, 10, 18, 19, 22, 23, 28
Wallace, Paul A. W., 4, 7, 9, 11, 19, 22, 23
Walla Walla Treaty, 35
War, French and Indian or Seven Years, 7, 9, 21, 22, 23, 27
War of Independence, see American Revolution
Warriors, see Men
Washburn, Wilcomb E., 27
Washington, George, 7
Washington State, or Territory, 33
Watkins, Arthur V., 29, 37, 43
Wayne, Anthony (U. S. general), 35
Webb, Walter Prescott, 43
Weepink (Delaware settlement), 13, 14
Weiser, Conrad (Pennsylvania interpretor), 11
Welfare, 21
Weslager, C. A., 4, 5, 15, 17, 18, 22, 38
Wharton State Forest, 11
White, Robert A., 24, 37
White(s) (man, people), see Anglo-American
Wilson, Edmund, 30
Winnebago Lake, 17, 18

Wisconsin, 18, 29, 38
Wish-fulfillment, see Dreams
Wishram (Indians), 30, 39
Wittfogel, Karl August, 30
Women, Anglo-American, 20, 26, 41
Women, Indian (and as a term for Delawares), 4, 8, 10, 18, 22–23, 26, 40
Wood, C. E. S., 28
Woodward, Major E. M., 16, 17

World War I, 35, 36
World War II, 29, 36
Wounded Knee, 36
Wyoming Valley, Pa., 8

Yahi (Indians), 27
Yakima (Indians), 28
Yale, 5

Yaple, Robert L., 7
Yaqui (Indians), 30, 38, 39
Yeoman, see Farmer

Zeisberger, David, 5
Zimmerman, Albright G., 19
Zimmerman, William Jr., 43

MEMOIRS
OF THE
AMERICAN PHILOSOPHICAL SOCIETY

Medical Men at the Siege of Boston, April, 1775–April, 1776: Problems of the Massachusetts and Continental Armies. PHILIP CASH.
Vol. 98. xiv, 185 pp., 11 figs., 1973. Paper. $3.00.

Crucial American Elections. ARTHUR S. LINK *et al.*
Vol. 99. x, 77 pp., 1973. $3.00.

John Beckley: Zealous Partisan in a Nation Divided. EDMUND BERKELEY and DOROTHY SMITH BERKELEY.
Vol. 100. xvi, 312 pp., 6 figs., 1973. $6.00.

Peter Tudebode: Historia de Hierosolymitano Itinere. JOHN HUGH HILL and LAURITA L. HILL.
Vol. 101. xii, 137 pp., 2 maps, 1974. $5.00.

Benjamin Franklin's Philadelphia Printing: A Descriptive Bibliography. C. WILLIAM MILLER.
Vol. 102. xc, 583 pp., illus., 1974. $40.00.

The Anschluss Movement in Austria and Germany, 1918–1919, and the Paris Peace Conference. ALFRED D. LOW.
Vol. 103. xiv, 495 pp., 4 figs., 4 maps, 1974. Paper. $8.00.

Studies in Pre-Vesalian Anatomy: Biography, Translations, Documents. L. R. LIND.
Vol. 104. xiv, 344 pp., 54 figs., 1975. $18.00.

A Kind of Power: The Shakespeare–Dickens Analogy. ALFRED B. HARBAGE. Jayne Lectures for 1974.
Vol. 105. x, 78 pp., 1975. $4.00.

A Venetian Family and Its Fortune, 1500–1900: The Donà and the Conservation of Their Wealth. JAMES C. DAVIS.
Vol. 106. xvi, 189 pp., 18 figs., 1975. $6.50.

Academica: Plato, Philip of Opus, and the Pseudo-Platonic Epinomis. LEONARDO TARÁN.
Vol. 107. viii, 417 pp., 1975. $20.00.

The Roman Catholic Church and the Creation of the Modern Irish State, 1878–1886. EMMET LARKIN.
Vol. 108. xiv, 412 pp., 2 figs., 1 map, 1975. Paper. $7.50.

Science and the Ante-Bellum American College. STANLEY M. GURALNICK.
Vol. 109. xiv, 227 pp., 1975. Paper. $5.00.

Hilary Abner Herbert: A Southerner Returns to the Union. HUGH B. HAMMETT.
Vol. 110. xvi, 264 pp., 20 figs., 1976. Paper. $5.00.

Census of the Exact Sciences in Sanskrit. Series A, Volume 3. DAVID PINGREE.
Vol. 111. vi, 208 pp., 1976. Paper. $15.00.

Cyriacus of Ancona's Journeys in the Propontis and the Northern Aegean, 1444–1445. EDWARD W. BODNAR and CHARLES MITCHELL.
Vol. 112. viii, 90 pp., 24 figs., 1976. Paper. $6.00.

The Autobiography of John Fitch. Edited by FRANK D. PRAGER.
Vol. 113. viii, 215 pp., 15 figs., 1976. Paper. $7.00.

TRANSACTIONS

OF THE

AMERICAN PHILOSOPHICAL SOCIETY

Gears from the Greeks: The Antikythera Mechanism—A Calendar Computer from *ca.* 80 B.C.   DEREK DE SOLLA PRICE.
Vol. 64, pt. 7, 70 pp., 45 figs., 1974. $5.00.

The Imperial Library in Southern Sung China, 1127–1279: A Study of the Organization and Operation of the Scholarly Agencies of the Central Government.   JOHN H. WINKELMAN.
Vol. 64, pt. 8, 61 pp., 8 figs., 1974. $5.00.

The Czechoslovak Heresy and Schism: The Emergence of a National Czechoslovak Church.   LUDVIK NEMEC.
Vol. 65, pt. 1, 78 pp., 1975. $6.00.

Distractions of Peace During War: The Lloyd George Government's Reactions to Woodrow Wilson, December, 1916–November, 1918.   STERLING J KERNEK.
Vol. 65, pt. 2, 117 pp., 1975. $6.00.

Classification and Development of North American Indian Cultures: A Statistical Analysis of the Driver-Massey Sample.   HAROLD E. DRIVER and JAMES L. COFFIN.
Vol. 65, pt. 3, 120 pp., 12 figs., 5 maps, 1975. $7.00.

The Flight of Birds.   CRAWFORD H. GREENEWALT.
Vol. 65, pt. 4, 67 pp., 41 figs., 1 pl., 1975. $7.00.

A Guide to Francis Galton's English Men of Science.   VICTOR L. HILTS.
Vol. 65, pt. 5, 85 pp., 6 figs., 1975. $5.00.

Justice in Medieval Russia: Muscovite Judgment Charters (*Pravye Gramoty*) of the Fifteenth and Sixteenth Centuries.   ANN M. KLEIMOLA.
Vol. 65, pt. 6, 93 pp., 1975. $5.00.

The Sculpture of Taras.   JOSEPH COLEMAN CARTER.
Vol. 65, pt. 7, 196 pp., 72 pls., 2 maps, 1975. $18.00.

The Franciscans in South Germany, 1400–1530: Reform and Revolution.   PAUL L. NYHUS.
Vol. 65, pt. 8, 47 pp., 1975. $3.00.

The German Center Party, 1890–1906.   JOHN K. ZEENDER.
Vol. 66, pt. 1, 125 pp., 2 figs., 1976. $7.50.

Perugia, 1260–1340: Conflict and Change in a Medieval Italian Urban Society.   SARAH RUBIN BLANSHEI.
Vol. 66, pt. 2, 128 pp., 2 maps, 1976. $8.50.

Crystals and Compounds: Molecular Structure and Composition in Nineteenth-century French Science.   SEYMOUR H. MAUSKOPF.
Vol. 66, pt. 3, 82 pp., 4 figs., 1976. $4.50.

The Bourgeois Democrats of Weimar Germany.   ROBERT A. POIS
Vol. 66, pt. 4, 117 pp., 1976. $6.00.

The Persecution of Peter Olivi.   DAVID BURR.
Vol. 66, pt. 5, 98 pp., 1976. $6.00

Gaetano Filangieri and His *Science of Legislation*.   MARCELLO MAESTRO.
Vol. 66, pt. 6, 76 pp., 4 figs. 1976. $6.00.

Recurrent Themes and Sequences in North American Indian-European Culture Contact.   EDWARD McM. LARRABEE.
Vol. 66, pt. 7, 52 pp., 6 figs., 3 maps, 1976. $6.00.